PROJECT: EARRINGS

KALMBACH BOOKS

MW00635242

Kalmbach Books
21027 Crossroads Circle
Waukesha, Wisconsin 53186
www.Kalmbach.com/Books

Published in 2012
16 15 14 13 12   1 2 3 4 5

Manufactured in the United States of America

ISBN: 978-0-87116-489-6
EISBN: 978-0-87116-757-6

The material in this book has appeared previously in *Bead&Button* magazine and the *Beading with Gemstones* special issue. *Bead&Button* is registered as a trademark.

Editor: Elisa R. Neckar
Art Director: Lisa Bergman
Technical Editor: Lesley Weiss
Designers: Rebecca Markstein, Lisa Schroeder, & Michael Soliday
Illustrator: Kellie Jaeger
Photographers: Jim Forbes & Bill Zuback

Library of Congress Cataloging-in-Publication Data

Project. Earrings / [compiled by Kalmbach Books].

    p. : ill. (some col.) ; cm.

    Issued also as an ebook.

    "44 designs using beads, wire, chain, and more"--Cover.

    "The material in this book has appeared previously in Bead&Button magazine."--T.p. verso.

    ISBN: 978-0-87116-489-6

    1. Earrings--Handbooks, manuals, etc. 2. Beadwork--Handbooks, manuals, etc. 3. Jewelry making--Handbooks, manuals, etc. I. Kalmbach Publishing Company. II. Title: Earrings III. Title: Bead&Button magazine.

TT860 .P76 2012

Contents

Introduction

Clearly whoever said that you can't have too much of a good thing was talking about earrings.

As beaders and jewelry makers know, there's no such thing as too many earrings — and *Project: Earrings* is proof of that. The wealth of projects included here represents the wide range of styles, materials, and techniques that can be combined to create beautiful baubles for your ears.

If you prefer the challenge of complex wire-wrapping projects, you'll love Sonia Kumar's stunning "Paisley perfection" (p. 80). Or maybe you've been searching for stitched earring projects — Virginia Jensen's "Spinner rims" (p. 56) will be just what you're looking for. Or maybe you just need a pair of earrings you can make quickly for a party tonight. Cathy Jakicic's "Tiny dancers" (p. 26) use only basic loop-making and stringing techniques to create charming dangles. The three sections that make up this book represent the variety of techniques that you can employ: loops and stringing, stitching, and wirework and chain mail.

Whatever the technique you choose, the 44 projects packed into these pages are sure to delight you with their style, versatility, and just plain fun. Can you really ever have enough earrings? *Project: Earrings* is here to help you try!

Tools & Materials

chainnose pliers

roundnose pliers

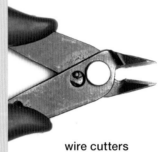

wire cutters

crimping pliers

split-ring pliers

Excellent tools and materials for making jewelry are available in bead and craft stores, through catalogs, and on the Internet. Here are the essential supplies you'll need for the projects in this book.

TOOLS

Chainnose pliers have smooth, flat inner jaws, and the tips taper to a point. Use them for gripping, bending wire, and for opening and closing loops and jump rings.

Roundnose pliers have smooth, tapered, conical jaws used to make loops. The closer to the tip you work, the smaller the loop will be.

Use the front of a **wire cutters'** blades to make a pointed cut and the back of the blades to make a flat cut. Do not use your jewelry-grade wire cutters on memory wire, which is extremely hard; use heavy-duty wire cutters, or bend the memory wire back and forth until it breaks.

Crimping pliers have two grooves in their jaws that are used to fold or roll a crimp bead into a compact shape.

Make it easier to open split rings by inserting the curved jaw of **split-ring pliers** between the wires.

Beading needles are coded by size. The higher the number, the finer the beading needle. Unlike sewing needles, the eye of a beading needle is almost as narrow as its shaft. In addition to the size of the bead, the number of times you will pass through the bead also affects the needle size that you will use. If you will pass through a bead multiple times, you need to use a thinner needle.

beading needles

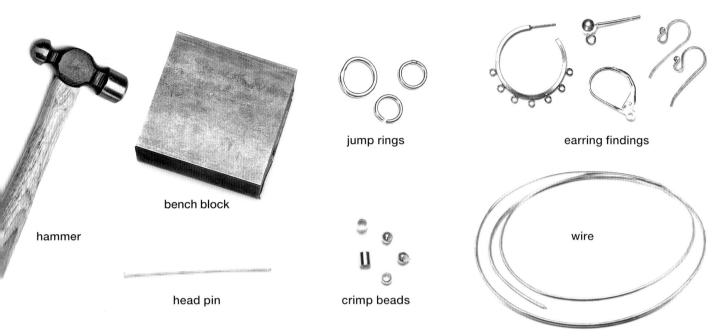

jump rings

earring findings

bench block

hammer

wire

head pin

crimp beads

A **hammer** is used to harden wire or texture metal. Any hammer with a flat head will work, as long as the head is free of nicks that could mar your metal. The light ball-peen hammer shown here is one of the most commonly used hammers for jewelry making.

A **bench block** provides a hard, smooth surface on which to hammer wire and metal pieces. An **anvil** is similarly hard but has different surfaces, such as a tapered horn, to help form wire into different shapes.

FINDINGS

A **head pin** looks like a long, blunt, thick sewing pin. It has a flat or decorative head on one end to keep beads on. Head pins come in different metals, diameters (or gauges), and lengths.

A **jump ring** is used to connect two loops. It is a small wire circle, oval, or decorative shape that is either soldered closed or comes with a split so you can twist the jump ring open and closed.

Crimp beads are large-hole, thin-walled metal beads designed to be flattened or crimped into a tight roll. Use them when stringing jewelry on flexible beading wire. **Crimp bead covers** provide a way to hide your crimps by covering them with a finding that mimics the look of a small bead.

Earring findings come in a huge variety of metals and styles, including post, French hook, hoop, and leverback. You will almost always want a loop (or loops) on earring findings so you can attach beads or beadwork.

WIRE

Wire is available in a number of materials and finishes, including brass, gold, gold-filled, gold-plated, fine silver, sterling silver, anodized niobium (chemically colored wire), and copper. Brass, copper, and craft wire are packaged in 10- to 40-yd. (9.1–37m) spools, while gold, silver, and niobium are sold by the foot or ounce. Wire thickness is measured by gauge — the higher the gauge number, the thinner the wire. It is available in varying hardnesses (dead-soft, half-hard, and hard) and shapes (round, half-round, square, and others).

STITCHING & STRINGING MATERIALS

Thread comes in many sizes and strengths. Size (diameter or thickness) is designated by a letter or number. OO, O, and A are the thinnest threads; B, D, E, F, and FF are subsequently thicker.

Plied gel-spun polyethylene (GSP), such as Power Pro or DandyLine, is made from polyethylene fibers that have been spun into two or more threads that are braided together. It is

almost unbreakable, doesn't stretch, and resists fraying. The thickness can make it difficult to make multiple passes through a bead. It is ideal for stitching with larger beads, such as pressed glass and crystals. **Parallel filament GSP**, such as Fireline, is a single-ply thread made from spun and bonded polyethylene fibers. Because it's thin and strong, it's best for stitching with small seed beads.

Other threads are available, including **parallel filament nylon**, such as Nymo or C-Lon, and **pre-conditioned parallel filament nylon**, like K.O. or One-G (best used in bead weaving and bead embroidery); **plied nylon thread**, such as Silamide (good for twisted fringe, bead crochet, and beadwork that needs a lot of body); and **polyester thread**, such as Gutermann (best for bead crochet or bead embroidery when the thread must match the fabric).

Flexible beading wire is composed of steel wires twisted together and covered with nylon. This wire is much stronger than thread and does not stretch. The higher the number of inner strands (between three and 49), the more flexible and kink-resistant the wire. It is available in a variety of sizes and colors. Use .014 and .015 for most gemstones, crystals, and glass beads. Use thicker varieties (.018, .019, and .024) for heavy beads or nuggets. Use thinner wire (.010 and .012) for lightweight pieces and beads with very small holes, such as pearls.

Tools & Materials

BEADS

Many of the projects in this book will call for **seed beads** as the main elements of the design. The most common and highest-quality seed beads are manufactured in Japan or the Czech Republic. These seed beads are the most uniform and predictable in size, shape, and hole size. Bead sizes are written as a number with a symbol, such as 11/0 or 11º (pronounced "eleven aught"). Sizes range from 2º (6mm) to 24º (smaller than 1mm) — the higher the number, the smaller the bead. The most common seed bead size is 11º, but most suppliers carry sizes ranging from 6º to 15º. Seed beads smaller than 15º are difficult to work with as their holes are tiny, and thus are rarely used and very hard to find.

Japanese cylinder beads, which are sold under the brand names Delicas, Treasures, or Aikos, are very consistent in shape and size. Unlike the standard round seed bead, they're shaped like little tubes and have very large, round holes and straight sides. They create an even surface texture when stitched together in beadwork. These beads are also sold in tubes or packages by weight. In addition to round and cylinder beads, there are several other seed bead shapes: **Hex-cut beads** are similar to cylinder beads, but instead of a smooth, round exterior, they have six sides. **Triangle beads** have three sides, and **cube beads** have four. **Bugle beads** are long, thin tubes that can range in size from 2 to 30mm long. You might also find tiny teardrop-shaped beads, called **drops** or **fringe drops**, and **magatamas**. Cube, drop, and bugle beads are sold by size, measured in millimeters (mm) rather than aught size.

Some projects may also use a variety of **accent beads** to embellish your pieces, including **crystals**, **gemstones**, **fire-polished beads**, and **pearls**, to name only a few types.

seed beads

cube beads

triangle beads

drop beads

twisted bugle beads

hex-cut beads

Czech seed beads

Techniques

THREAD AND KNOTS

Adding thread

To add a thread, sew into the beadwork several rows or rounds prior to the point where the last bead was added, leaving a short tail. Follow the thread path of the stitch, tying a few half-hitch knots (see "Half-hitch knot") between beads as you go, and exit where the last stitch ended. Trim the short tail.

Conditioning thread

Use beeswax or microcrystalline wax (not candle wax or paraffin) or Thread Heaven to condition nylon beading thread and Fireline. Wax smooths nylon fibers and adds tackiness that will stiffen your beadwork slightly. Thread Heaven adds a static charge that causes the thread to repel itself, so don't use it with doubled thread. Both conditioners help thread resist wear. To condition, stretch nylon thread to remove the curl (Fireline doesn't stretch). Lay the thread or Fireline on top of the conditioner, hold it in place with your thumb or finger, and pull the thread through the conditioner.

Ending thread

To end a thread, sew back through the last few rows or rounds of beadwork, following the thread path of the stitch and tying two or three half-hitch knots (see "Half-hitch knot") between beads as you go. Sew through a few beads after the last knot, and trim the thread.

Stop bead

Use a stop bead to secure beads temporarily when you begin stitching. Choose a bead that is different from the beads in your project. Pick up the stop bead, leaving the desired length tail. Sew through the stop bead again in the same direction, making sure you don't split the thread. If desired, sew through it one more time for added security.

Half-hitch knot

Pass the needle under the thread bridge between two beads, and pull gently until a loop forms. Cross back over the thread between the beads, sew through the loop, and pull gently to draw the knot into the beadwork.

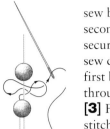

Overhand knot

Make a loop with the thread. Pull the tail through the loop, and tighten.

Square knot

[1] Cross one end of the thread over and under the other end. Pull both ends to tighten the first half of the knot.
[2] Cross the first end of the thread over and under the other end. Pull both ends to tighten the knot.

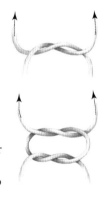

Surgeon's knot

[1] Cross one end of the thread over and under the other twice. Pull both ends to tighten the first half of the knot.
[2] Cross the first end of the thread over and under the other end. Pull both ends to tighten the knot.

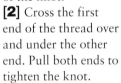

Brick stitch

[1] To work the typical method, which results in progressively decreasing rows, work the first row in ladder stitch (see "Ladder stitch") to the desired length, exiting the top of the last bead added.
[2] Pick up two beads, sew under the thread bridge between the second and third beads in the previous row, and

sew back up through the second bead added. To secure this first stitch, sew down through the first bead and back up through the second bead.

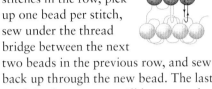

[3] For the remaining stitches in the row, pick up one bead per stitch, sew under the thread bridge between the next two beads in the previous row, and sew back up through the new bead. The last stitch in the new row will be centered above the last two beads in the previous row, and the new row will be one bead shorter than the previous row.

Increasing

To increase at the start of the row, repeat step 1 above, then repeat step 2, but sew under the thread bridge between the first and second beads in the previous row. To increase at the end of the row, work two stitches off of the thread bridge between the last two beads in the previous row.

Crossweave technique

Crossweave is a beading technique in which you string one or more beads on both ends of a length of thread or cord and then cross the ends through one or more beads.

Herringbone stitch
Flat

[1] Work the first row in ladder stitch (see "Ladder stitch") to the desired length, exiting the top of an end bead in the ladder.
[2] Pick up two beads, and sew down through the next bead in the previous row (a–b). Sew up through the following bead in the previous row, pick

up two beads, and sew down through the next bead (b–c). Repeat across the first row.
[3] To turn to start the next row, sew down through the end bead in the previous row and back through the last bead of the pair just added (a–b). Pick up two beads, sew down through the next bead in the previous row, and sew up through the following bead (b–c). Continue adding pairs of beads across the row.

Tubular

[1] Work a row of ladder stitch (see "Ladder stitch") to the desired length using an even number of beads. Form it into a ring to create the first round (see "Ladder stitch: Forming a ring"). Your thread should exit the top of a bead.
[2] Pick up two beads, sew down through the next bead in the previous round (a–b), and sew up through the following bead. Repeat to complete the round (b–c).
[3] You will need to step up to start the next round. Sew up through two beads — the next bead in the previous round and the first bead added in the new round (c–d).
[4] Continue adding two beads per stitch. As you work, snug up the beads to form a tube, and step up at the end of each round until your rope is the desired length.

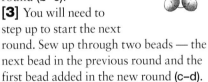

Ladder stitch
Making a ladder

[1] Pick up two beads, and sew through them both again, positioning the beads side by side so that their holes are parallel (a–b).
[2] Add subsequent beads by picking up one bead, sewing through the previous bead, then sewing through

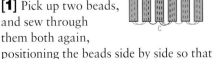

the new bead (b–c). Continue for the desired length. This technique produces uneven tension, which you can correct by zigzagging back through the beads in the opposite direction or by choosing the "Crossweave method" or "Alternative method."

Crossweave method
[1] Thread a needle on each end of a length of thread, and center a bead.
[2] Working in crossweave technique, pick up a bead with one needle, and cross the other needle through it (a–b and aa–bb). Add all subsequent beads in the same manner.

Alternative method
[1] Pick up all the beads you need to reach the length your project requires. Fold the last two beads so they are parallel, and sew through the second-to-last bead again in the same direction (a–b).

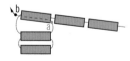

[2] Fold the next loose bead so it sits parallel to the previous bead in the ladder, and sew through the loose bead in the same direction (a–b). Continue sewing back through each bead until you exit the last bead of the ladder.

Forming a ring
With your thread exiting the last bead in the ladder, sew through the first bead and then through the last bead again. If using the "Crossweave method" or "Alternative method" of ladder stitch, cross the threads from the last bead in the ladder through the first bead in the ladder.

Peyote stitch
Flat even-count
[1] Pick up an even number of beads, leaving the desired length tail

(a–b). These beads will shift to form the first two rows as the third row is added.
[2] To begin row 3, pick up a bead, skip the last bead added in the previous step, and sew back through the next bead, working toward the tail (b–c). For each stitch, pick up a bead, skip a bead in the previous row, and sew through the next bead until you reach the first bead picked up in step 1 (c–d). The beads added in this row are higher than the previous rows and are referred to as "up-beads."
[3] For each stitch in subsequent rows, pick up a bead, and sew through the next up-bead in the previous row (d–e). To count peyote stitch rows, count the total number of beads along both straight edges.

Tubular
Tubular peyote stitch follows the same stitching pattern as flat peyote, but instead of sewing back and forth, you work in rounds.
[1] Start with an even number of beads tied into a ring (see "Square knot").
[2] Sew through the first bead in the ring. Pick up a bead, skip a bead in the ring, and sew through the next bead. Repeat to complete the round.
[3] To step up to start the next round, sew through the first bead added in round 3 (a–b). Pick up a bead, and sew through the next bead in round 3 (b–c). Repeat to complete the round.
[4] Repeat step 3 to achieve the desired length, stepping up after each round.

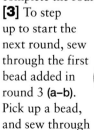

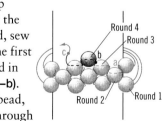

Circular
Circular peyote is worked in continuous rounds like tubular peyote, but the rounds stay flat and radiate outward from the center as a result of increasing the number of beads per stitch or using larger beads. If the number or size of the beads is not sufficient to fill the spaces between stitches, the circle will not lie flat.

Right-angle weave
Flat strip
[1] To start the first row of right-angle weave, pick up four beads, and tie them into a ring (see "Square knot"). Sew through the first three beads again.
[2] Pick up three beads. Sew through the last bead in the previous stitch (a–b), and continue through the first two beads picked up in this stitch (b–c).
[3] Continue adding three beads per stitch until the first row is the desired length. You are stitching in a figure-8 pattern, alternating the direction of the thread path for each stitch.

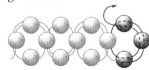

Adding rows
[1] To add a row, sew through the last stitch of row 1, exiting an edge bead along one side.

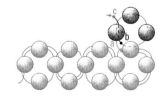

[2] Pick up three beads, and sew through the edge bead your thread exited in the previous step (a–b). Continue through the first new bead (b–c).

[3] Pick up two beads, and sew back through the next edge bead in the previous row and the bead your thread exited at the start of this step (a–b). Continue through the two new beads and the following edge bead in the previous row (b–c).

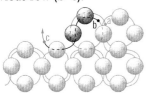

[4] Pick up two beads, and sew through the last two beads your thread exited in the previous stitch and the first new bead. Continue working a figure-8 thread path, picking up two beads per stitch for the rest of the row.

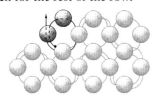

Whip stitch

Use whip stitch to join two layers of fabric with a finished edge.

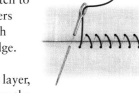

[1] Sew up through one layer, and cross over the edges diagonally about 1/16 in. (2mm) from where your thread is exiting.
[2] Sew down through both layers diagonally, exiting about 1/16 in. (2mm) from where your thread exited at the start of step 1.
[3] For each subsequent stitch, cross over the edges diagonally, and sew down through both edges as in step 2.

STRINGING & WIREWORK

Crimping

Use crimp beads to secure flexible beading wire. Slide the crimp bead into place, and squeeze it firmly with chainnose pliers to flatten it. For a more finished look, use crimping pliers.

[1] Position the crimp bead in the hole that is closest to the handle of the crimping pliers.
[2] Holding the wires apart, squeeze the pliers to compress the crimp bead, making sure one wire is on each side of the dent.
[3] Place the crimp bead in the front hole of the pliers, and position it so the dent is facing the tips of the pliers. Squeeze the pliers to fold the crimp in half.

Opening and closing loops and jump rings

[1] Hold a loop or a jump ring with two pairs of pliers, such as chainnose, flatnose, or bentnose pliers.
[2] To open the loop or jump ring, bring the tips of one pair of pliers toward you, and push the tips of the other pair away from you. Reverse the steps to close.

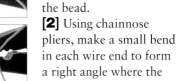

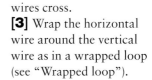

Plain loop

[1] Using chainnose pliers, make a right-angle bend in the wire directly above a bead or other component or at least 1/4 in. (6mm) from the end of a naked piece of wire. For a larger loop, bend the wire further in.
[2] Grasp the end of the wire with roundnose pliers so that the wire is flush with the jaws of the pliers where they meet. The closer to the tip of the pliers that you work, the smaller the loop will be. Press downward slightly, and rotate the wire toward the bend made in step 1.
[3] Reposition the pliers in the loop to continue rotating the wire until the end of the wire touches the bend.

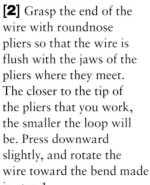

Wraps above a top-drilled bead

[1] Center a top-drilled bead on a 3-in. (7.6cm) piece of wire. Bend each wire end upward, crossing them into an X above the bead.
[2] Using chainnose pliers, make a small bend in each wire end to form a right angle where the wires cross.
[3] Wrap the horizontal wire around the vertical wire as in a wrapped loop (see "Wrapped loop"). Trim the excess wrapping wire.
[4] If desired, make a wrapped loop (see "Wrapped loop") with the vertical wire directly above the wraps.

Wrapped loop

[1] Using chainnose pliers, make a right-angle bend in the wire about 2mm above a bead or other component or at least 1 1/4 in. (3.2cm) from the end of a naked piece of wire.
[2] Position the jaws of the roundnose pliers in the bend. The closer to the tip of the pliers that you work, the smaller the loop will be.
[3] Curve the short end of the wire over the top jaw of the roundnose pliers.
[4] Reposition the pliers so the lower jaw fits snugly in the loop. Curve the wire downward around the bottom jaw of the pliers. This is the first half of a wrapped loop.
[5] To complete the wraps, grasp the top of the loop with one pair of pliers.
[6] With another pair of pliers, wrap the wire around the stem two or three times. Trim the excess wire, and gently press the cut end close to the wraps with chainnose pliers.

Sparkling loops

MATERIALS

- **6** 6mm faceted pearls
- **8** 5mm bicone crystals
- **30** 4mm bicone crystals
- **8** 4mm round pearls
- **52** 1-in. (2.5cm) 22-gauge head pins
- **3** in. (7.6cm) cable chain
- pair post earring findings with loops and ear nuts
- **2** 3mm jump rings
- chainnose pliers
- roundnose pliers
- wire cutters

String multiple sizes of crystals with pearls and chain for quick and easy hoops with dazzling sparkle

designed by **Anna Elizabeth Draeger**

These quick earrings use only a small number of beads, making them a perfect project for leftovers.

stepbystep

[1] Cut the chain in half, making sure the two pieces of chains have an equal number of links (the earrings shown above use 14 links). Open the loop (Basics) on an earring finding, attach the end link of one of the chains, and close the loop **(photo a)**.

[2] String a crystal on a head pin and make a plain loop (Basics) above the crystal. Repeat with the remaining crystals and pearls.

[3] Open the loop on one 4mm bicone crystal dangle and attach it to the loop on the post earring finding **(photo b)**.

[4] Attach the remaining dangles as follows: two 4mm bicones to the second link; a 4mm round pearl and a 5mm bicone crystal to the third link; and a 6mm faceted pearl to the fourth link **(photo c)**. Repeat the bead sequence, ending with a 4mm round pearl and a 5mm bicone crystal on the last link.

[5] Open a jump ring (Basics) and connect the last link to the ear nut **(photo d)**.

[6] Make a second earring using the remaining dangles.

Crystal trio

Three colors of crystals and dangles of varying lengths add interest to contemporary earrings

designed by **Kristin Schneidler**

MATERIALS

- 4mm bicone crystals:
  - **6** color A
  - **8** color B
  - **10** color C
- **6** 1½-in. (3.8cm) head pins
- pair of earring findings
- chainnose pliers
- roundnose pliers
- wire cutters

When you mix three crystal colors, sometimes one dominates, as the amber does in this set. For jewelry with meaning, choose three colors that have significance for you, such as the birthstones of your family members.

stepbystep

[1] Trim a head pin to 1 in. (2.5cm), a second head pin to 1¼ in. (3.2cm), and a third head pin to 1½ in. (3.8cm).
[2] String three color A crystals on the 1-in. (2.5cm) head pin, four color B crystals on the 1¼-in. (3.2cm) head pin, and five color C crystals on the 1½-in. (3.8cm) head pin.

[3] Make a plain loop (Basics) at the end of each head pin (photo a).
[4] Open the loop of an earring finding (Basics), attach the head pin units, positioning the longest one in the middle, and close the loop (photo b).
[5] Make a second earring.

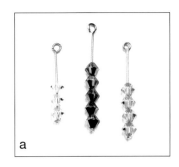

a

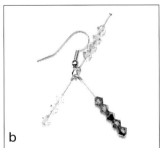

b

Chalcedony
drops

Copper, gemstones, and leather make ruggedly pretty earrings

designed by **Addie Kidd**

The gemstone chalcedony occurs naturally in shades of white, gray, black, light to dark green (called chrysoprase), and lavender. The classic light blue used in these earrings makes a lovely contrast with the soft brown leather and copper beads.

a

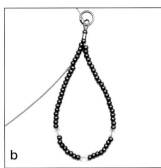
b

c

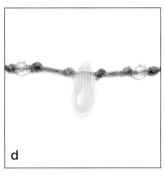
d

FIGURE

e

f

g

MATERIALS

- **2** 12mm faceted green chalcedony briolettes, top drilled
- **12** 3mm fire-polished crystals
- **3g** 11º hollow metal seed beads, matte copper plated
- flexible beading wire, .018 or .019
- **1 ft.** (30cm) Irish waxed linen cord, 0.5mm, 4-ply
- **2 ft.** (61cm) lightweight suede lacing, 2mm
- **2** 6mm split rings
- **2** crimp beads
- pair of earring findings
- chainnose pliers
- crimping pliers (optional)
- roundnose pliers
- wire cutters
- G-S Hypo Cement
- head pin, T-pin, or awl

EDITOR'S NOTE:

The waxed linen cord is too thick to be doubled on a needle and pulled through beads. Create a temporary beading tip by flattening the cord with pliers. Using sharp scissors, cut the tip at an angle and roll it into a point. When the fibers begin to separate, repeat.

stepbystep

[1] Cut a 16-in. (41cm) piece of beading wire, and string an 11º seed bead, a crimp bead, 23 11ºs, a 3mm fire-polished crystal, eight 11ºs, a 3mm, eight 11ºs, a 3mm, and 22 11ºs. Go back through the first three beads strung **(photo a)**.

[2] On one end, string a split ring and go back through the top three beads and six 11ºs on one side. Leaving a small loop for the split ring, tighten the wire **(photo b)**.

[3] On the same working wire, string six 11ºs, a 3mm, and six 11ºs. Go up through the last six beads on the opposite side and through the top three beads **(photo c)**. Adjust the loops and tighten the wire. Crimp the crimp bead (Basics), and trim the tails.

[4] Cut a 6-in. (15cm) piece of waxed linen cord, and center a briolette on it. Tie an overhand knot (Basics) on each side of the briolette. Tie another knot ³⁄₁₆ in. (5mm) from the knot. On each end, string a 3mm on each side and tie another knot **(photo d)**.

[5] Fold the cord in half. To make a half-hitch knot around the top of the earring, pass both cord ends through the split ring, around the beaded wires and cord, and through the loop just made at the back **(figure)**. Adjust the cord so the briolette hangs centered just above the lower wire loop, and tighten the knot **(photo e)**. Make another half-hitch knot around the beaded wires and cord.

[6] Cut a 12-in. (30cm) piece of suede. Holding a 5-in. (13cm) tail along the length of the earring, go through the split ring from front to back. Without twisting the suede, wrap tightly for approximately ½ in. (1.3cm) around the beaded wires, cords, and tail, overlapping slightly. Tie a square knot with the tails at the back of the earring **(photo f)**. Dot the knot with glue. At the end of each tail, tie an overhand knot just below the bottom wire loop. Leave approximately ⅛ in. (3mm) of tail below each knot, and trim.

[7] Open the loop of an earring finding (Basics), attach the split ring, and close the loop **(photo g)**.

[8] Make a second earring.

Cup-chain conundrum

designed by **Anna Elizabeth Draeger**

MATERIALS
- 2 yd. (1.8m) 24-gauge craft wire to match findings
- 12 in. (30cm) 2mm crystal cup-chain
- 2 ⅜ in. (1cm) mesh domes with post earring backs
- chainnose pliers
- wire cutters

Mesh findings define the shape of sparkling earrings with lots of movement

Drawn to the flash of rhinestones, Anna knew she had to have earrings like these when they caught her eye at an antique shop. Unfortunately, closer inspection revealed that some of the crystals had darkened over time, tarnishing her excitement. To replicate the design, Anna called on Diane Hyde for the perfect mesh findings and added crystal cup-chain to complete her dazzling earrings.

Look for interesting shapes to turn any mesh finding into a glittering accessory. Cup-chain also comes in a variety of sizes.

a

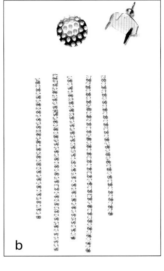

b

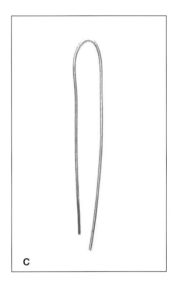

c

stepbystep

[1] Decide on your desired design, and carefully cut the cup-chain apart with wire cutters (photo a). Each of these earrings uses two 2-in. (5cm) pieces, two 2½-in. (6.4cm) pieces, and one 2¼-in. (5.7cm) piece of cup-chain.

[2] Lay out the chains, making sure the design is wide enough to cover the mesh finding (photo b).

[3] Cut the 24-gauge wire into 14 2-in. (5cm) sections. Bend the wires in half (photo c).

[4] Hold the 2¼-in. (5.7cm) cup-chain section up to the middle of the mesh finding. Slide the wire ends through two adjacent holes of the

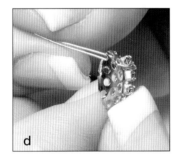

d

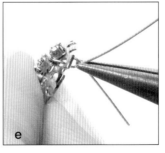

e

f

mesh finding from front to back, straddling the cup-chain between two cups (photo d). Cross the wires in the back of the mesh finding.

[5] Using chainnose pliers, twist the wire to snug the cup-chain up to the mesh finding (photo e). Leaving a ⅛-in. (3mm) piece of twisted wire, trim the wire. Bend the twisted wire over to lie flat against the back of the mesh finding.

[6] Keeping the cup-chain as straight as possible, attach it to the mesh finding between the next two cups. Repeat to secure the cup-chain across the surface of the mesh finding.

[7] Position a 2-in. (5cm) section of cup-chain next to the first chain, and repeat the wiring process. Continue to attach the remaining cup-chains in the same manner. Try not to wire the cup-chain

too close to the edge of the mesh finding, as it will make it very difficult to attach the back of the finding.

[8] When all of the chains are attached, align the earring back with the mesh finding, and use chainnose pliers to bend the prongs over the front (photo f). (You may need to cut the prongs a little bit to get them to lie properly.)

[9] Make a second earring.

Parisian nights

The distinctive materials in these earrings will set you apart from the crowd

designed by **Ann Dee Allen**

MATERIALS

- 2 18mm large-hole Swarovski crystals
- 2 6mm round copper beads
- 10 8º bronze seed beads
- 2 16mm filigree bead caps
- 7 in. (18cm) 22-gauge vintage bronze wire
- 12 in. (30cm) decorative brass chain, 2mm links
- pair of brass earring findings
- chainnose pliers
- roundnose pliers
- wire cutters

The bronzy tones of vintage-style chain and filigree complement a faceted crystal bead.

stepbystep

[1] Cut a 1½-in. (3.8cm) piece of wire, and make a plain loop (Basics).

[2] Cut three 1¾-in. (4.4cm) pieces of chain. Open the plain loop (Basics), and attach a center link of each chain so that the two ends hang down. Close the loop.

[3] String five 8º seed beads, an 18mm crystal, and a filigree bead cap **(photo)**. Snug up the bead cap, crystal, and plain loop, hiding the seed beads inside the crystal. Make a plain loop.

[4] Cut a 1¾-in. (4.4cm) piece of wire, and make a wrapped loop (Basics). String a 6mm copper bead, and make a wrapped loop.

[5] Open the plain loop at the top of the crystal unit, and attach it to one of the wrapped loops. Close the loop. Open the loop of an earring finding, and attach it to the other wrapped loop. Close the loop.

[6] Make a second earring.

Emeralds & pearls

Emerald rondelles sparkle against white coin pearls

designed by **Lynne Soto**

a

b

c

For millennia, the emerald has been the stone of royalty and is considered a stone of harmony, wisdom, and love. Pairing tiny emerald green rondelles with pearls certainly creates sweet harmony!

stepbystep

[1] On 12 in. (30cm) of Fireline, pick up a 12mm coin pearl and 10 2mm rondelles, leaving a 6-in. (15cm) tail. Make a surgeon's knot (Basics) at the base of the 12mm **(photo a)**.
[2] Sew back through the 12mm. Thread a needle on the tail, and sew back through the 12mm. Trim the threads.

[3] On a head pin, string a 5mm freshwater pearl, the embellished 12mm, and a 5mm. Make a wrapped loop (Basics) **(photo b)**.
[4] Open the loop of an earring finding (Basics). Attach the dangle and close the loop **(photo c)**.
[5] Make a second earring.

EDITOR'S TIP:
The holes in the 2mm rondelles may be too small to allow even a size 15 needle to pass through, so you may need to string the rondelles without a needle on the Fireline.

MATERIALS
- 2 12mm coin pearls
- 4 5mm freshwater pearls
- 20 2mm emerald rondelles
- Fireline, 6 lb. test, crystal
- 2 3-in. (7.6cm) head pins
- pair of earring wires
- chainnose pliers
- roundnose pliers
- wire cutters
- beading needles, #15

Moment in time

Cage crystals in filigree for ageless elegance

designed by **Kathy Budda**

a

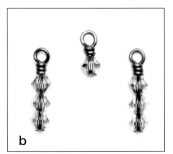

b

c

d

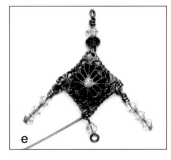

e

f

The beauty of making earrings is that you get your beading fix with time to spare. In this pair, shimmering crystal buttons peek through components that evoke the past.

stepbystep

[1] On an eye pin, string a 4–6mm saucer or rondelle and a 4mm bicone crystal. Make a wrapped loop (Basics) **(photo a)**.

[2] To make a dangle, string three bicones on a head pin, and make a wrapped loop. Repeat to make a second dangle. Make a third dangle using one bicone **(photo b)**.

[3] Open the bottom loop (Basics) of the bead unit from step 1. Hold two filigree components together so the right sides face out. This will make a space in which the crystal button will sit. Slide the filigrees' top openings into the loop of the bead unit. Close the loop **(photo c)**.

[4] Open a jump ring, and attach a three-crystal dangle. Slide the jump ring through corresponding openings on one side of the filigrees, and close the jump ring **(photo d)**. Repeat on the other side of the filigree.

[5] Slide the crystal button between the two filigrees.

[6] On an eye pin, string a bicone, and make the first half of a wrapped loop.

Attach the bottom openings of the filigrees **(photo e)**, and complete the wraps.

[7] Open the loop of the eye pin attached in the previous step, and attach the single-crystal dangle **(photo f)**. Close the loop.

[8] Open the loop of an earring finding, attach the wrapped loop at the top of the earring, and close the loop.

[9] Make a second earring.

Can't-beat copper earrings

A hardware-store staple goes glam with texture and a no-fuss patina

designed by **Kimberly Berlin**

MATERIALS

- at least 6 in. (15cm) copper tubing, ¼–⅜-in. (6mm–1cm) diameter
- **4–6** 6–8mm metal, gemstone, or crystal rondelles, round beads, or bicone beads
- **4** 11º seed beads
- 7 in. (18cm) 22-gauge wire (optional)
- **2** 2-in. (5cm) head pins
- pair of earring findings
- bench block or anvil
- clear, non-yellowing satin urethane spray for metals, such as Minwax Helmsman Spar Urethane Clear Satin spray or Rust-Oleum Ultra Cover Satin clear spray
- metal file
- permanent marker in the color of your choice
- polishing cloth or paper towel
- scrap flexible beading wire
- texture hammer, cross-peen hammer, or ball-peen hammer
- wire clothes hanger
- chainnose pliers
- roundnose pliers
- tube-holding or tube-cutting pliers (optional)
- tube cutter
- wire cutters

DESIGNER'S NOTES:

- Hammering too hard in step 1 could cause the tubing to collapse.
- If using a file to texture the tubing, larger file grooves will produce a rougher texture, which will show the marker better.
- If you are using tubing finer than ¼ in. (6mm), use a jeweler's saw to cut the tubing. Also, consider using tube-cutting pliers (like the ones shown in **photo b**). They have a slit through the jaws to accommodate the saw blade.

Fine-gauge tubing may be too delicate to hammer, but it makes for a smooth and dainty version of these earrings.

With silver and gold prices still inflated, it's smart to harvest copper tubing from your local hardware store. Texture and trim the metal to make tube beads, then have some fun coloring to create a patina in the recesses. Now you're set to string simple earrings!

stepbystep

[1] Place one end of the tubing on a bench block or anvil. Using a texture hammer or the peen (back end) of a cross-peen or ball-peen hammer, gently strike the end of the tubing to texture the metal **(photo a)**. Hammer up to ¼–½ in. (6mm–1.3cm) from the end, then slowly rotate the tubing to texture all the way around. Reposition the tubing on the bench block or anvil to add texture from another direction. Alternatively, file the tubing with even strokes to create a subtle texture.
[2] Using tube-holding pliers, tube-cutting pliers, or your fingers, grasp the tubing above the texture. Place the tubing in the tube cutter so the blade is positioned at the end of the texture. Tighten the screw of the cutter until the blade touches the tubing **(photo b)**, then tighten the screw a quarter turn more.
[3] Holding the tubing still, rotate the tube cutter twice around the tubing. You should notice the blade scoring the surface of the metal. Tighten the screw a quarter turn more, and repeat. Continue tightening the screw and rotating the cutter until the end of the tubing falls off. File the ends of the textured tube.
[4] Color the textured tube with a permanent marker **(photo c)**, then quickly rub it off with a polishing cloth or paper towel, leaving the color in the

a

b

c

texture marks. Color the ends of the tube if desired.

[5] Repeat steps 1–4 to make a second textured tube bead.

[6] String a tube bead on a piece of scrap beading wire, and tie the ends of the wire together. Repeat with the other bead. String each beading wire loop over the neck of a clothes hanger, and arrange the beads so they do not touch. In a well-ventilated area, evenly spray the beads with clear satin urethane. This seals the copper, protecting it from oxidation. Let the beads dry overnight.

[7] For a short earring dangle: On a head pin, string an 11º seed bead, a 6–8mm bead, a tube bead, a 6–8mm bead, and an 11º seed bead. Make a

wrapped loop (Basics). Open the loop of an earring finding (Basics), attach the wrapped loop, and close the loop.

For a longer earring dangle: On a head pin, string a 6–8mm bead, and make a wrapped loop. Cut a 3½-in. (8.9cm) piece of 22-gauge wire, and make the first half of a wrapped loop. Slide the dangle into the loop, and complete the wraps. String a 6–8mm bead, a tube bead, and a 6–8mm bead, and make a wrapped loop. Open the loop of an earring finding, attach the top wrapped loop, and close the loop.

[8] Repeat step 7 to make a second earring.

EDITOR'S NOTES:

To avoid marring the metal in step 2, place a small square of non-slip drawer liner in the jaws before grasping the tubing.

Clusters & vines

Modernize the classic pairing of jade and cloisonné with a design that resembles a vining tendril

designed by **Julia Gerlach**

MATERIALS
- **6** 6mm jade beads
- **12** 5mm jade beads
- **8** 4mm round crystals
- **10** 3mm bicone crystals
- **1g** 15º gold-plated seed beads
- Fireline 6 lb. test
- pair of earring findings
- chainnose pliers
- roundnose pliers
- beading needles, #12

Primarily mined in China, jade is said to promote peace, strength, creativity, and mental agility. Gold-plated seed beads add to the lush look of the verdant gemstones and accompanying crystals.

DESIGNER'S NOTE:
Many inexpensive stones called "jade" are available on the market. Most of these are actually dyed quartz, serpentine, or marble. For a budget-minded option, try combining one of these with Czech fire-polished glass instead of crystals.

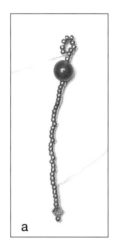
a

b

c

stepbystep

[1] On 24 in. (61cm) of Fireline, pick up ten 15º seed beads, and tie them into a ring with a square knot (Basics). Sew through the 15ºs twice, then pick up a 15º, a 5mm jade bead, 30 15ºs, a 3mm crystal, and a 15º. Skip the last 15º, and sew back through the 3mm and five 15ºs (photo a).

[2] Pick up a 3mm and a 15º, and sew back through the 3mm and four 15ºs on the stem. Pick up a 4mm crystal and a 15º, and sew back through the 4mm and three 15ºs on the stem. Pick up a 5mm jade and a 15º, and sew back through the 5mm and two 15ºs on the stem **(photo b)**.

[3] Make a dense cluster of beads by adding a crystal or jade bead after each 15º, as in step 2. Use 6mm in the middle to make the cluster a bit wider in the center. End the threads (Basics).

[4] Open the loop of an earring finding (Basics), attach the dangle, and close the loop **(photo c)**. Make a second earring.

Playing the angles

Crystal spacers add light and definition

designed by **Anna Elizabeth Draeger**

Two-hole spacers make convenient brackets for columns of sparkling crystals in this easy earring ensemble.

MATERIALS

- **14** 6mm bicone crystals
- **4** two-hole 11 x 5mm crystal spacer bars
- **2** in. (5cm) fine chain
- **4** 22-gauge head pins
- pair of earring findings
- roundnose pliers
- chainnose pliers
- wire cutters

a

b

c

stepbystep

[1] String a crystal on a head pin. Repeat. String a spacer bar over both head pins.
[2] String a crystal on one of the head pins and two crystals on the other. String a second spacer bar.
[3] String a crystal on each head pin **(photo a)**.
[4] Trim each head pin, leaving ¼ in. (6mm) of wire above the top bead, and make a plain loop (Basics).

[5] Cut the chain in half. If this doesn't leave an odd number of links, remove links as needed.
[6] Open the loop of one head pin (Basics), and attach an end link of chain. Close the loop. Repeat on the other head pin **(photo b)**.
[7] Open the loop of an earring finding, and attach the middle chain link. Close the loop **(photo c)**.
[8] Make a second earring.

Swingy chandeliers

Link components to make wearable mini chandeliers

designed by **Bethany Heywood**

These dimensional earrings look complex, even though they don't take very long to make. And unlike flat chandelier designs, these links form a dynamic structure that looks good from all angles.

MATERIALS

- fire-polished beads
  - **2** 8mm round
  - **12** 6mm round
  - **12** 5 x 7mm teardrop
  - **16** 4mm round
- **8** 4mm round pearls
- **8** 1½-in. (3.8cm) 24-gauge head pins
- **32** 1½-in. (3.8cm) 24-gauge eye pins
- pair of earring findings
- chainnose pliers
- roundnose pliers
- wire cutters

stepbystep

Components

[1] On a head pin, pick up a teardrop bead and a 4mm pearl. Make a plain loop (Basics and **photo a**). Repeat to make a total of four A dangles.

[2] Using eye pins, make the following links with plain loops (**photo b**):
- one B link, using 8mm beads
- six C links, using 6mm beads
- two D links, using teardrop beads
- eight E links, using 4mm beads

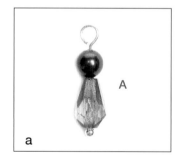

Assembly

[1] Open a loop of a C link (Basics). Attach two E links, and close the loop (**photo c**).

[2] Continue connecting links as in step 1 to make a chain of four C and four E links (**photo d**). Make sure all the C links hang down on the same side.

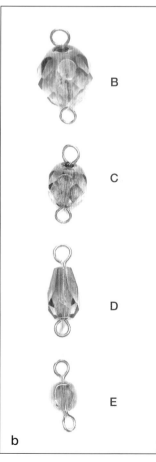

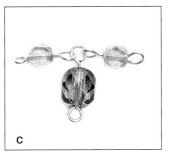

c

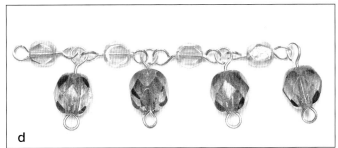

d

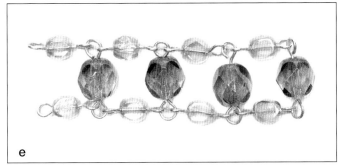

e

f

g

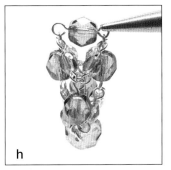

h

i

j

[3] Use four E links to connect the unattached loops of the C links, forming a ladder (photo e).

[4] To connect the ladder into a cube, connect the unattached loops of the end E links to the loops of the end C link (photo f).

[5] Attach a loop of a B link to a loop of a C link, in between the E-link loops. Attach the B link's other loop to the loop of the C link at the opposite corner of the cube (photo g).

[6] Turn the cube over, and locate a loop of a C link that isn't connected to the B link. Attach a new C link to that loop. Attach the new C link's other loop to the loop of the C link at the opposite corner of the cube (photo h).

[7] Attach the bottom loop of a D link to a loop of the B link. Attach another D link to the B link's other loop.

[8] Attach an earring finding to a C link. Attach the C link's other loop to the top loop of each of the D links (photo i).

[9] Attach A dangles to the bottom four corners of the earring, connecting two to the bottom loops of the vertical C links and connecting the other two to the loops of the horizontal C link (photo j).

[10] Make a second earring.

DESIGNER'S NOTES:

Using the bead sizes in the materials list as a guideline, try other creative combinations of beads. If your beads are too small, stack two or more on one head pin or eye pin, like the green rondelles used in place of the C links in this pair.

Tiny dancers

Tiny rondelles sparkle along with equally delicate silver accents

designed by **Cathy Jakicic**

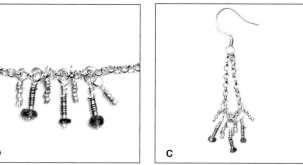

MATERIALS

- **6** 2–4mm sapphire rondelles
- **6** 3.5mm Hill Tribes silver tube beads
- **24–32** 1mm round Hill Tribes silver spacers
- **4** in. (10cm) cable chain, 2–3mm links
- **14** 1½-in. (3.8cm) head pins
- pair of earring findings
- chainnose pliers
- roundnose pliers
- wire cutters

Some early civilizations thought the sky was an enormous sapphire in which the Earth was embedded. While the thought of a gem of that size is truly impressive, it's nice to know that even the smallest sapphires are beautiful enough to inspire a little awe.

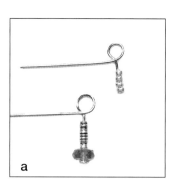

a

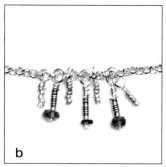

b

c

stepbystep

[1] On a head pin, string a sapphire rondelle and a tube bead. Make the first half of a wrapped loop (Basics). Make a total of three sapphire units. On a head pin, string

three or four 1mm spacers **(photo a)**. Make the first half of a wrapped loop. Make a total of four spacer units.
[2] Cut a 2-in. (5cm) piece of chain. Attach the sapphire and spacer units to the center of the chain, leaving one link

open between each unit. Complete the wraps **(photo b)**.
[3] Open the loop of an earring finding (Basics) and attach the end links of the chain. Close the loop **(photo c)**.
[4] Make a second earring.

EDITOR'S NOTE:

When you're using a graduated strand, position it in a channel of a bead design board and cut the strand in the middle. This will keep the beads in order by size and let you access both the largest and smallest beads.

DESIGN NOTE:

To save money, substitute sapphire crystal rondelles for the sapphires and silver-plated findings for the Hill Tribes and sterling silver.

Beadwoven beauties

Amber ovals look dramatic against a backdrop of black seed beads

designed by **Lynne Soto**

MATERIALS

- **6** 11 x 4mm oval amber beads
- **22** 8º seed beads
- **58** 11º seed beads
- pair of earring findings
- Nymo D beading thread
- beading needles, #12

Amber is fossilized tree resin, so it's no surprise that it's found around the world. The gemstone's light weight and saturated colors, ranging from golden yellow to cherry red, have made it a favorite of jewelry makers for thousands of years.

stepbystep

[1] On 1 yd. (.9m) of thread, leave a 10-in. (25cm) tail, and pick up an 8º seed bead, an oval amber bead, three 11º seed beads, an oval, an 8º, and three 11ºs (figure, a–b). Sew back through the 8º and oval to form a bead picot (b–c).

[2] Pick up three 11ºs, an oval, two 8ºs, seven 11ºs, an 8º, three 11ºs, two 8ºs, and three 11ºs (c–d). Sew back through the single 8º (d–e).

[3] Pick up seven 11ºs and an 8º (e–f). Sew through the first 8º picked up in step 1, the oval, and the three 11ºs (f–g).

[4] Thread a needle on the tail. Pick up three 8ºs (h–i). Sew through the 8º next to the oval, the oval, and three 11ºs (i–j).

[5] At points **g** and **j**, cross the threads and retrace the opposite thread paths. Return to points **g** and **i**. Tie a square knot, and end the threads (Basics).

[6] Open the loop of an earring wire (Basics). Attach the earring, positioning the earring wire between the two top 8ºs. Close the loop.

[7] Make a second earring.

FIGURE

Touch of paradise

Embellish curving earrings with graduated accent bead spikes

designed by **Glenda Paunonen**

The fun, fringy curves of these earrings can be bold or delicate, and call to mind the pointed plumes often sported by tropical birds or exotic flowers. Each pair of earrings uses only a handful of beads, making this a great project for leftovers.

stepbystep

[1] On 1 yd. (.9m) of thread, pick up four 11º seed beads, leaving a 6-in. (15cm) tail. Tie the beads into a ring with a square knot (Basics), and sew through the first 11º again.

[2] Picking up three 11ºs per stitch, work 20 stitches in right-angle weave (Basics). Sew through the last three beads again.

[3] Pick up an 11º, a 6mm accent bead, and an 11º. Skip the last 11º, and sew back through the 6mm and the first 11º. Continue through the next edge 11º in the strip (figure, a–b).

[4] Repeat step 3 five times, using each type of accent bead in descending sizes: type

A 4mm, type B 4mm, type A 3mm, type B 3mm, and 10º triangle or 2mm (b–c).

[5] Sew through the 11º in the center of the strip and the next 11º on the opposite edge (c–d).

[6] Repeat steps 3–5 twice, ending by sewing through the top 11º in the strip (d–e).

[7] Sew through the next seven 11ºs on the edge of the strip, then through the next 11º in the center of the strip, pulling the beads snug (e–f). Repeat twice, but do not sew through the bottom 11º (f–g).

[8] Pick up nine 11ºs, skip the next seven edge beads, and sew through the next 11º in the center of the strip (g–h). Repeat twice (h–i).

[9] Pick up five 11ºs, and sew through the 11º your

MATERIALS

- 6 6mm accent beads
- 6 4mm accent beads, in each of **2** types: A, B
- 6 3mm accent beads, in each of **2** types: A, B
- 6 10º triangle beads or 2mm accent beads
- 4g 11º seed beads
- pair of earring findings
- nylon beading thread, size D
- beading needles, #12
- bentnose pliers
- chainnose pliers

thread exited at the start of this step (i–j). Retrace the thread path through the loop, secure the working thread and tail in the beadwork with a few half-hitch knots (Basics), and trim.

[10] Open the loop (Basics) of an earring finding, attach the loop at the top of the earring, and close the loop.

[11] Make a second earring, attaching it to the earring finding as the mirror image of the first.

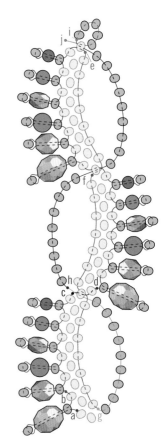

FIGURE

Beaded bead caps

A variety of stitches equals multiple design options

designed by **Amy Johnson**

MATERIALS

- 2 ¾-in. (1.9cm) art-glass beads
- crystals
  - **2** 8mm rondelles
  - **2** 6mm bicones
  - **8** 4mm bicones, color A
  - **6** 4mm bicones, color B
- **12** 4mm crystal pearls
- 1–2g 11º Japanese cylinder beads
- 2g 15º seed beads
- **2** 2-in. (5cm) 22-gauge head pins
- pair of earring findings
- Fireline 6 lb. test
- beading needles, #12 or #13
- chainnose pliers
- roundnose pliers
- wire cutters

These coin-shaped beads support the beaded bead caps well, but other shapes would also work.

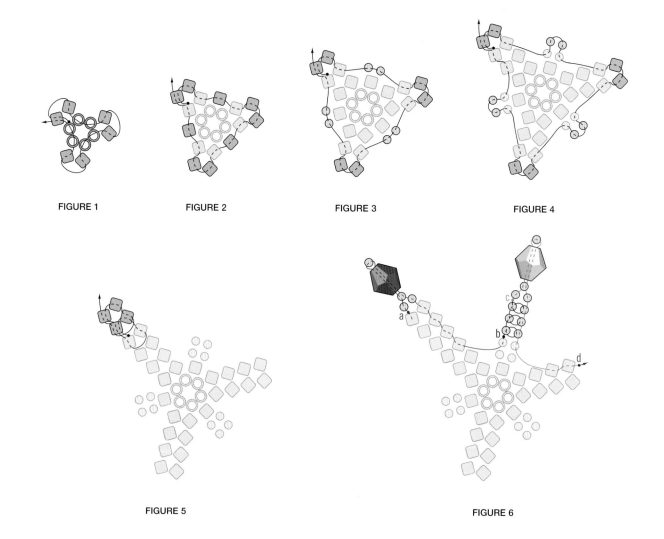

FIGURE 1

FIGURE 2

FIGURE 3

FIGURE 4

FIGURE 5

FIGURE 6

Amy Johnson's earrings show that simple, beautiful design can result from utilizing more than one technique. She built her "Rain Forest Earrings" around Rita Stucke's lampworked beads using ladder stitch, herringbone, square stitch, and fringe. They are a great project for learning to stitch beads.

stepbystep

Base

[1] On 2 yd. (1.8 m) of Fireline, make a six-bead ladder (Basics) using cylinder beads and leaving a 12-in. (30cm) tail. Join the ladder into a ring (Basics) to form round 1.

[2] Work in herringbone stitch (Basics) as follows:

Round 2: Pick up two cylinders, and sew through the next two cylinders in the ring. Repeat twice, and step up through the first cylinder in the new round (figure 1).

Round 3: Work an increase herringbone round: Pick up two cylinders, and sew down through the next cylinder in the previous round. Pick up a cylinder, and sew up through the next cylinder in the previous round. Repeat twice, and step up through the first cylinder in the new round (figure 2).

Round 4: Work another increase herringbone round: Pick up two cylinders, and sew down through the next cylinder in the previous round. Pick up two 15º seed beads, and sew up through the next cylinder in the previous round. Repeat twice, and step up through the first cylinder in the new round (figure 3).

Round 5: Pick up two cylinders, and sew down through the next cylinder in the previous round and up through the next 15º. Pick up two 15ºs, and sew down through the next 15º in the previous round and up through the next cylinder. Repeat twice, and step up through the first cylinder in the new round (figure 4).

Bottom fringe

[1] To make a cylinder fringe, pick up two cylinders, sew through the next cylinder and the cylinder your thread exited at the start of this step, and continue through the first cylinder just added. Repeat once (figure 5).

[2] Add a crystal embellishment to the end of the cylinder fringe: Pick up two 15ºs, a color A 4mm bicone, and a 15º. Skip the last 15º, and sew back through the A and one 15º. Pick up a 15º, and sew through the next four cylinders in the column. Sew through the next 15º in the same round (figure 6, a–b).

[3] To make a 15º fringe: Pick up two 15ºs, and sew through the next 15º. Sew

DESIGNER'S NOTE:

For earrings with a little more sparkle, instead of picking up seven 15°s in step 2 of "Edge trim," pick up a 15º, a 3mm pearl, a 3mm Czech glass bead, and a 15º. Skip the last 15º, and sew through the rest of the beads. Then, instead of picking up five 15ºs, pick up a 15º, a 4mm crystal, and a 15º. Skip the last 15º, and sew back through the 4mm and the 15º.

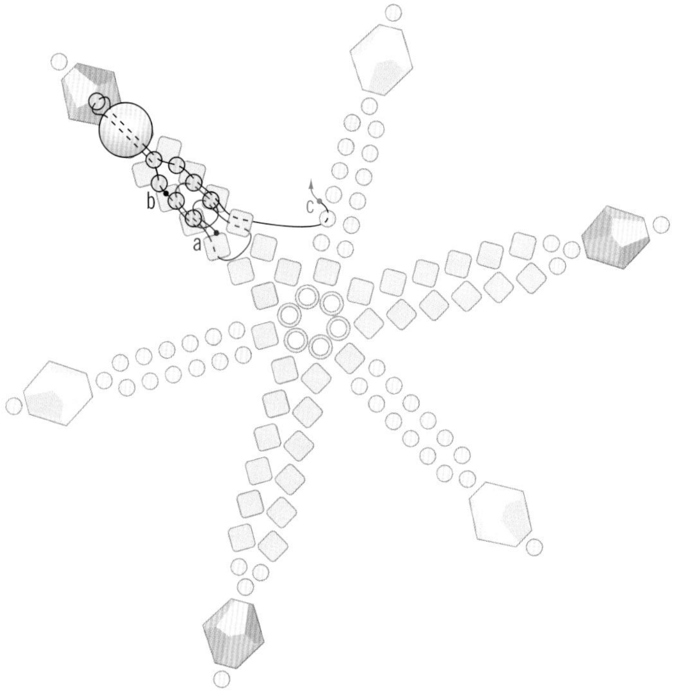

FIGURE 7

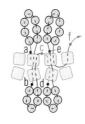

FIGURE 8

through the 15º your thread exited at the start of this step and the first 15º added. Repeat twice **(b–c)**.

[4] Add a crystal embellishment at the end of the 15º fringe: Pick up two 15ºs, a color B 4mm bicone, and a 15º. Sew back through the B and one 15º. Pick up a 15º, and sew through the next four 15ºs in the column. Sew through the last two cylinders in the next column **(c–d)**.

[5] Repeat steps 1–4 twice, but in the last repeat of step 4, sew through five 15ºs in the column. Sew through the next cylinder in the same round.

Top fringe

The top round of fringe is worked in the same manner as the bottom fringe, off the pairs of cylinders and 15ºs established in the bottom fringe.

[1] Pick up two 15ºs, and sew through the next cylinder in the previous round and the cylinder your thread exited at the start of this step. Sew through the first new 15º added. Repeat once **(figure 7, a–b)**.

[2] Pick up two 15ºs, a 4mm pearl, and a 15º, and sew back through the pearl and one 15º. Pick up a 15º, and sew through the next two 15ºs and a cylinder in the same column. Sew through the next 15º in the same round **(b–c)**.

[3] Repeat steps 1 and 2, but in step 2, sew through three 15ºs instead of two 15ºs and a cylinder, and sew through the next cylinder in the round instead of a 15º.

[4] Repeat until you have six top fringes, and end the working thread (Basics).

Edge trim

[1] Thread a needle on the tail, and make sure the thread is exiting round 1 pointing away from the fringe **(figure 8, point a)**. The edge trim will be added to each cylinder in the ladder at the very top of the bead cap and to the pairs of cylinders in the first increase round.

[2] Pick up seven 15ºs, sew back through the cylinder your thread exited at the start of this step, and continue through the cylinder below it **(figure 8, a–b)**. Pick up five 15ºs, and sew back through the same two base cylinders **(b–c)**. Sew through the next two cylinders in the base **(c–d)**. Pick up five 15ºs, and sew back through the two cylinders your thread just exited **(d–e)**. Pick up seven 15ºs, and sew back through the last cylinder your thread exited, and the next cylinder in round 1 **(e–f)**.

[3] Repeat step 2 until you have completed six loops off of rounds 1 and 2. End the tail.

Assembly

[1] On a head pin, string an A, an 8mm rondelle, an art-glass bead, the beaded bead cap, a 6mm bicone crystal, and a 15º.

[2] Make a plain loop (Basics) above the cylinder.

[3] Open the loop (Basics), and attach an earring finding. Close the loop.

[4] Make a second earring.

Kaleidoscope connection

Connect a collection of kaleidoscopic components for a colorful earrings

designed by **Julie Olah**

Brick stitch and circular peyote connect for fun earrings that work up quickly.

MATERIALS

- 8 6º seed beads
- 2g 11º seed beads, in each of 4 colors: A, B, C, D
- pair of earring findings
- 3 9mm split rings or soldered jump rings
- Fireline 6 lb. test, or nylon beading thread, size D
- beading needles, #10 or #12

stepbystep

Open circle

[1] On 1 yd. (.9m) of Fireline or thread, pick up a 9mm split ring or soldered jump ring and two color A 11º seed beads, leaving a 6-in. (15cm) tail. Position the As side by side around the outside of the ring, sew through the ring, and sew back through the second A **(figure 1, a–b)**. (For tips on keeping the first A in place, see the Editor's Note, p. 33.)

[2] Working in brick stitch (Basics), pick up an A, sew through the split ring or soldered jump ring as if it is a thread bridge, and sew back through the A just added **(b–c)**.

[3] Repeat step 2 around the split ring or soldered jump ring to add about 14 As.

[4] When you reach the first A added, sew down through it, through the split ring or soldered jump ring, and back through the A **(figure 2)**.

[5] Pick up two color B 11º seed beads, sew under the thread bridge connecting the first two As in the previous round,

and sew back through the second B **(figure 3, a–b)**.

[6] Pick up a B, and sew under the next thread bridge and back through the B **(b–c)**.

[7] Continue working in brick stitch, adding one or two Bs per thread bridge to make the second round of Bs fit snugly around the first round of As. Tie a few half-hitch knots (Basics), but do not trim the working thread. End the tail (Basics).

[8] Make a second open circle.

Patterned circles

[1] On 1 yd. (.9m) of Fireline or thread, pick up five As, and tie them into a ring with a square knot (Basics), leaving a 6-in. (15cm) tail. Sew through the first A again **(figure 4, a–b)**.

[2] Pick up a B, and sew through the next A in the ring **(b–c)**. Repeat around, and step up through the first B added **(c–d)**.

[3] Working in circular peyote stitch (Basics), pick up two color C 11º seed

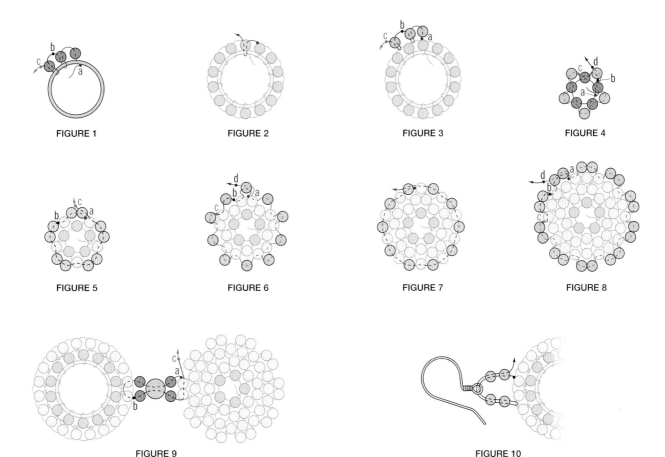

FIGURE 1　　FIGURE 2　　FIGURE 3　　FIGURE 4

FIGURE 5　　FIGURE 6　　FIGURE 7　　FIGURE 8

FIGURE 9　　FIGURE 10

beads, and sew through the next B (figure 5, a–b). Repeat around, and step up through the first C added (b–c).

[4] Pick up a color D 11º seed bead, and sew through the next C (figure 6, a–b). Pick up a B, and sew through the next C (b–c). Repeat around, alternating Ds and Bs, and step up through the first D added (c–d).

[5] Work a round of circular peyote stitch, adding a C for each stitch, and step up through the first C added (figure 7).

[6] Pick up two Bs, and sew through the next C (figure 8, a–b). Pick up two Cs, and sew through the next C (b–c). Repeat around, alternating between two Bs and two Cs, and step up through the first pair of Bs added (c–d). Tie a few half-hitch knots, but do not trim the working thread. End the tail.

[7] Make a second patterned circle.

Assembly

[1] With your working thread exiting a pair of 11ºs in a patterned circle, pick up an 11º in the color of your choice, a 6º seed bead, and an 11º in the color of your choice. Sew through an 11º in round 2 of an open circle and the adjacent 11º in the round (figure 9, a–b). Pick up an 11º in the color of your choice, and sew back through the 6º. Pick up an 11º in the color of your choice, and sew through the pair of 11ºs your thread exited at the start of this step (b–c). Retrace the thread path to reinforce the connection, and end the thread.

[2] Exit the opposite side of the open circle. Pick up two 11ºs, the loop of an earring finding, and two 11ºs. Sew under the thread bridge between the next two beads on the circle and back up through the beads just added (figure 10). Retrace the thread path and end the threads.

[3] Assemble the second earring to match the first.

EDITOR'S NOTE:

To keep the first A 11º seed bead added in step 1 of "Open circle" in place while you work the first round, try one of the following:

- Hold it in place with your thumb.
- Tie the tail to the 9mm split ring or soldered jump ring.
- Add just one A in step 1, and anchor it by sewing through the split ring or soldered jump ring and back up through the A.

Star
power

Use this charming star component four different ways to create eye-catching accessories

designed by **Glorianne Ljubich**

EDITOR'S NOTES:
• Peanut beads may also be called butterfly beads, dogbones, or farfalle.
• Use a contrasting color for the center ring of beads to emphasize the floral look of the component.
• Substitute 4mm pearls, bicone crystals, or gemstone beads for fire-polished beads.

MATERIALS
• **36** 4mm fire-polished beads
• 2g 2 x 4mm peanut beads
• 2g 11º seed beads
• 2g 15º seed beads
• pair of earring findings
• Fireline 6 lb. test
• beading needles, #12

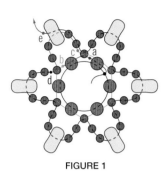

FIGURE 1

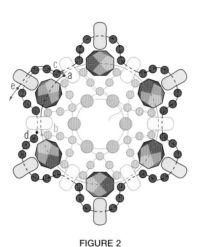

FIGURE 2

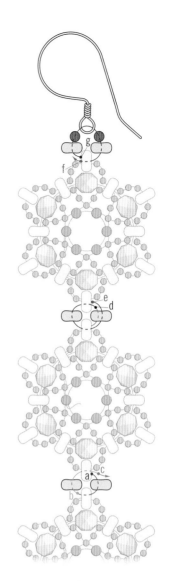

FIGURE 3

These components resemble tiny stars, but contrasting colors in the rings of beads can also create a floral look for your earrings.

stepbystep

[1] On 18 in. (46cm) of Fireline, pick up six 11° seed beads, and tie them into a ring with a square knot (Basics), leaving a 6-in. (15cm) tail. Sew through the first 11°.

[2] Pick up a 15° seed bead, and sew through the next 11° in the ring (figure 1, a–b). Repeat around the ring, and step up through the first 15° added in this round (b–c).

[3] Pick up two 15°s, a 2 x 4mm peanut bead, and two 15°s, and sew through the next 15° in the previous round (c–d). Repeat to complete the round, and step up through the first two 15°s and peanut bead added in this round (d–e).

[4] Pick up a 4mm fire-polished bead, and sew through the next peanut bead in the previous round (figure 2, a–b). Repeat to complete the round, exiting the peanut bead your thread exited at the start of this step (b–c).

[5] Pick up three 15°s, a peanut bead, and three 15°s, and sew through the next peanut bead in the previous round (c–d). Repeat to complete the round, and step up through the first three 15°s and peanut bead added in this round (d–e).

[6] Retrace the thread path, and tie a couple of half-hitch knots, but do not trim the working thread or tail.

[7] Repeat steps 1–6 to make a total of six large star components.

[8] With the working thread exiting a peanut bead in the outer round of one component, pick up a peanut bead, sew through the corresponding peanut bead on another component (figure 3, a–b), pick up a peanut bead, and sew through the peanut bead your thread exited at the start of this step (b–c). Retrace the thread path several times, and end the working thread and tail (Basics).

[9] Repeat step 2 to join the second component to a third component, being sure to make this connection opposite the first one (d–e).

[10] Using the working thread of the third component, sew through the beadwork to exit a peanut bead opposite the joining peanut beads (point f). Pick up a peanut bead, an 11°, the loop of an earring finding, an 11°, and a peanut bead, and sew through the peanut bead your thread exited at the start of this step (f–g). Retrace the thread path, and end the working thread and tail.

[11] Make a second earring.

The variety of available freshwater or Swarovski pearls will tempt you to create your own look.

Pearls in a pod

Add fresh peas to your jewelry diet

designed by **Jennifer Schwartzenberger**

a

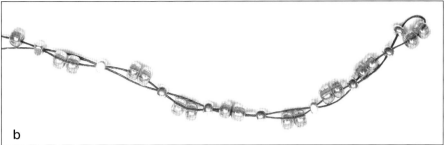

b

This earring design started as a twisted herringbone rope. Jennifer wasn't satisfied with the results, she says, "So I took it apart and discovered a pea pod had been hiding in there all along."

stepbystep

[1] On 1 yd. (.9m) of Fireline, attach a stop bead (Basics), leaving a 6-in. (15cm) tail. Pick up four color A 11º seed beads, and sew through all four beads again. Working in ladder stitch (Basics), make a two-bead ladder that is six stacks long.

[2] Form the ladder into a ring by sewing through the first and last stacks **(photo a)** and snugging up the stacks. Sew through the first stack again. You will start and end the rounds on the back side of the pea pod.

[3] Work in modified herringbone stitch (Basics) as follows:

Round 1: Pick up four As, and sew down through the next A in the ring and up through the following A **(figure 1, a–b)**. Pick up two As, a pearl, and two As, and sew down through the next A and up through the following A **(b–c)**. Pick up four As, and sew down through the next A **(c–d)** and up through the top three As in the first stack **(d–e)**. The needle is now positioned at the top of the first stack.

Round 2: Work a stitch with four As **(e–f)**. Pick up two As, sew through the pearl from round 1, pick up two As, and sew down through the next A and up through the following A **(f–g)**. Pick up four As, and sew down through the next A and up through the top three As of the first stack **(g–h)**.

Rounds 3–6: Repeat rounds 1 and 2 twice.

Rounds 7–8: Repeat rounds 1 and 2, but omit the pearl. Note: In round 7, the As will make an almost straight line across the top of the last pearl. The round 8 will pull the As back into the stacked alignment to mimic the first rounds.

[4] Close up the top by sewing through the beads in the last row as follows: Exit stack 1, and sew down through the top bead of stack 4 **(figure 2, a–b)** and up through the top bead of stack 5 **(b–c)**. Sew down through the top bead of stack 2 **(c–d)**, up through the top bead of stack 3 **(d–e)**, down through the top bead of stack 6 **(e–f)**, and up through stack 1 **(f–g)**.

[5] Pick up four As, and sew down through a few beads in stack 4 to create a loop.

Retrace the thread path to reinforce the loop. Sew through the beadwork to position the thread at the front of the pod.

[6] To make the curly vine, pick up a color B 11º seed bead, a 15º seed bead, two Bs, and a 15º. Repeat the pattern of two Bs and a 15º until you have 26 beads.

[7] Skipping the Bs, sew back through the 15ºs **(photo b)**. Pull the working thread to form curls.

[8] Secure the thread in the beadwork with a few half-hitch knots (Basics), and trim.

[9] Remove the stop bead. Thread a needle on the tail, and close up the beadwork as in step 4. Secure the thread, and trim.

[10] Open the loop (Basics) of an earring finding, and attach it to the bead loop. Close the loop.

[11] Repeat steps 1–10 to make a second earring.

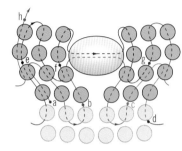

FIGURE 1

FIGURE 2

STITCHING

EDITOR'S NOTE:
Don't stop with just three of these adorable pea pods. Use five or six pearls to create longer earrings, or stitch several pods to make a fun necklace.

Lemon
squeezy

Color, texture, and pattern come together for sunny, summery dangles

designed by **Jane Danley Cruz**

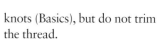

Stitch quick-and-easy netted bezels to encase rivolis, add crystals, and snap! You have beautiful dangles for a pair of earrings.

stepbystep

Rivoli bezel

[1] Thread a needle on each end of 2 ft. (61cm) of Fireline. With one needle, pick up a color B 15º seed bead and three color A 15º seed beads. Repeat 11 times.

[2] With the other needle, pick up three As, a B, and three As. Skip eight beads,

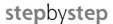

and sew through the next B added in step 1 (figure 1, a–b).

[3] Pick up three As, a B, and three As. Skip seven beads, and sew through the next B (b–c). Repeat three times (c–d). Pick up three As, a B, and three As.

[4] With one needle, sew through the first B added in step 1 to form a ring, and step up through the next three As and a B (figure 2, a–b).

[5] With the other needle, sew through the first B added in step 1, and step up through the next three As and a B opposite the beads you sewed through in step 4 (aa–bb).

[6] Designate one needle to work the top of the bezel and one to work the bottom. With the bottom needle, pick up

two Bs, skip seven beads in the previous round, and sew through the next B. Repeat to complete the round, and snug up the beads. Sew through the ring of Bs, and end the thread (Basics).

[7] Insert the 14mm rivoli, and hold it in place. With the top needle, sew through the back to exit a B. Pick up two Bs, skip seven beads in the previous round, and sew through the next B. Repeat to complete the round, using firm tension. Sew through the final ring of Bs.

[8] Sew through the beadwork to exit a B along the edge of the rivoli (figure 3, point a). Pick up a B, a 3mm bicone crystal, and a B, and sew through the next edge B (a–b). Repeat to complete the round (b–c). Retrace the thread path, tying a couple of half-hitch

knots (Basics), but do not trim the thread.

[9] Make another rivoli bezel.

Assembly

[1] With the thread exiting an edge B, pick up a repeating pattern of an A and a B twice, then pick up an A, a 3mm, a B, one side of a wire guard, and the loop of an earring finding.

[2] Center the loop of the earring finding on the wire guard, sew through the other side of the wire guard, and sew back through the last B, 3mm, and A. Pick up a repeating pattern of a B and an A twice. Skip a B, a 3mm, and a B on the bezel, and sew through the next edge B on the bezel. Retrace the thread path, and end the thread.

[3] Repeat steps 1 and 2 for the other rivoli bezel.

MATERIALS

- 2 14mm rivolis
- 14 3mm bicone crystals
- 1g 15º seed beads in each of 2 colors: A, B
- pair of earring findings
- 2 wire guards
- Fireline 6 lb. test
- beading needles, #12

FIGURE 1

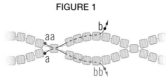

FIGURE 2

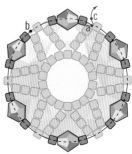

FIGURE 3

Add
it up

**Pairs of embroidered
components make
beautiful earrings**

designed by **Sherry Serafini**

Dress up your fringe with
daggers, drops, or disks.

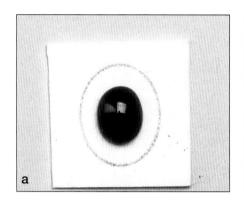

a

b

c

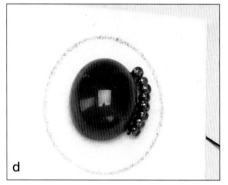

d

e

f

MATERIALS

- **2** 10–20mm cabochons
- **2** 8–12mm cabochons
- **30–100** assorted beads: 2–4mm daggers, drop beads, crystals, fire-polished beads, gemstones, pearls, or top-drilled beads
- 1–3g 8º seed beads
- 1–3g 11º seed beads
- 1–3g 15º seed beads
- pair of earring post findings
- nylon beading thread, size B, conditioned with beeswax or Thread Heaven
- beading needles, #12
- 4 x 4 in. (10 x 10cm) beading foundation
- E6000 adhesive
- 4 x 4 in. (10 x 10cm) Ultrasuede

Bead embroidery offers both freedom and a challenge in making a multitude of shapes with tiny beads. These bold designs feature long fringe with daggers, freshwater pearls, and Czech beads; you can make your earrings as elegant or as funky as you like.

stepbystep

Embroidered components
Preparation
[1] Determine how much beadwork will surround the cabochon, and draw the basic shape with a pencil on a piece of beading foundation.
[2] Glue a cabochon to the center of the beading foundation **(photo a)**, and let it dry.

Bezel
[1] Tie an overhand knot (Basics) at one end of 2 yd. (1.8m) of conditioned thread (Basics), and sew up through the beading foundation from back to front next to the cabochon.
[2] Work in beaded backstitch: Pick up four 15º seed beads, and stretch the thread along the beading foundation close to the cabochon. Sew down through the foundation right after the fourth 15º. Sew up through the foundation between the second and third 15ºs **(photo b)**. Sew through the third and fourth 15ºs again, and pick up four 15ºs **(photo c)**. Repeat **(photo d)** around the cabochon to create the base round, and end with an even number of beads.
[3] Pick up a 15º, skip a 15º in the base round, and sew through the next 15º **(photo e)**. Continue around in tubular peyote stitch (Basics), and step up through the first 15º added in this round **(photo f)**. If needed, work an additional round.
[4] Sew through the beadwork to exit the beading foundation on the back, and sew up through the foundation next to the peyote bezel.

Embellishment
[1] Using 15º or 11º seed beads, work a round of beaded backstitch close to the bezel.

40

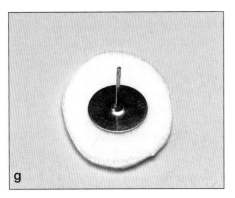

[2] Continue working in beaded backstitch to create the rest of your design using 8º seed beads, drop beads, pearls, fire-polished beads, crystals, gemstones, or other assorted beads.

[3] When you are satisfied with the design, end the thread (Basics). Trim the beading foundation close to the beadwork, making sure you don't cut the thread.

[4] Make a second bigger or smaller component to coordinate with the first.

Assembly

Back

[1] Glue an earring post finding to the back of the smaller component (photo g), and let it dry.

[2] Cut a piece of Ultrasuede the size of the smaller component, and pierce a hole for the post. Glue the Ultrasuede to the smaller component, pushing the stem of the earring finding through the hole (photo h). Let it dry.

[3] Cut a piece of Ultrasuede the size of the bigger component, and glue the Ultrasuede to the component. Let it dry.

[4] Carefully trim the Ultrasuede close to the beadwork.

[5] Repeat with the remaining components.

Edging

[1] Tie an overhand knot at the end of 1½ yd. (1.4m) of conditioned thread. Sew between the beading foundation and Ultrasuede at the edge of a component, and bring the needle up through the top of the beading foundation, hiding the knot between the two pieces.

[2] Pick up a 15º, sew down through the beading foundation and Ultrasuede, and sew back up through the 15º.

[3] Repeat step 2 around the component. When you reach the first 15º added, sew through it. Sew through a few beads in the embroidered beadwork, and tie a few half-hitch knots (Basics), but do not trim the thread.

[4] Repeat steps 1–3 to add edging to the remaining components.

Connecting components

[1] Determine where you want the smaller component to connect to the bigger component, and sew through the beadwork to exit a 15º at that location in the edging.

[2] Pick up a combination of 15ºs, 11ºs, 8ºs, or other assorted beads, and sew through the corresponding 15º in the edging of the other component. Sew through the next edge 15º, and repeat.

[3] Add as many connectors as desired. Photos i and j show two options.

[4] Retrace the thread path a couple of times, and sew through the beadwork to exit an edge 15º at the bottom of the bigger component.

Fringe

[1] Pick up an assortment of beads ending with four 15ºs; a dagger, drop bead, or top-drilled bead; and four 15ºs. Skip the last nine beads, and sew back through all the rest of the beads just added. Sew through the next edge 15º, and repeat to add fringe as desired, keeping your tension lax so the fringe will drape. Photo k shows a close-up of one fringe pattern.

[2] To make a strand to drape across the front of the fringe, sew through the next bottom edge 15º. Pick up an assortment of beads, drape the strand across the front of the fringe, and sew through the corresponding edge 15º on the other side (photo l). Retrace the thread path, and end the threads.

[3] Make a second earring.

Hexagonal
pillows

Dangle traditional Chinese hexagonal pillows from a pair of handmade earring findings

designed by **Valerie Hector**

If desired, patinate the completed pillows or the loose components with liver of sulfur following the manufacturer's instructions. Then gently shine them with a polishing cloth to add depth and contrast.

Making these structures in two pieces and joining the edges is easier than making the sphere as a whole, as is traditionally done.

stepbystep

Hexagonal pillows
Front and back halves

[1] Center a needle on 1 yd. (.9m) of thread or Fireline, and condition the doubled length of thread with beeswax (Basics). If you are using Fireline, waxing is optional.

[2] Pick up six 3mm round beads, and tie the beads into a ring with a surgeon's knot (Basics), leaving a 3-in. (7.6cm) tail. Sew through the next 3mm in the ring (figure 1).

[3] Begin the second round by picking up five 3mms, and sewing through the 3mm your thread exited and the next 3mm in the original ring (figure 2).

[4] Pick up four 3mms, and sew through the first 3mm added in the previous stitch, the 3mm your thread exited at the start of this step, and the next 3mm in the original ring (figure 3).

[5] Repeat step 4 three times, and sew through the last 3mm added in the first stitch of this round (figure 4).

[6] Pick up three 3mms, and sew through the last 3mm added in the previous stitch, the next 3mm in the original ring, and the next three 3mms in the first stitch of this round (figure 5).

MATERIALS

- **292** 3mm round beads
- **4** 5mm diameter bead caps
- **8 in.** (20cm) round 21-gauge sterling silver wire
- **2** 1 x 2mm crimp beads
- nylon beading thread, size D, or Fireline 6 lb. test
- beeswax (optional)
- beading needles, #10 and #12
- metal file
- oxidizing medium for silver such as liver of sulfur (optional)
- pencil or ¼-in. (6mm) dowel
- polishing cloth (optional)
- chainnose pliers
- roundnose pliers
- wire cutters

FIGURE 1   FIGURE 2

FIGURE 3   FIGURE 4   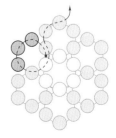FIGURE 5

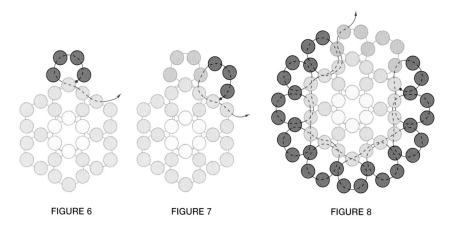

FIGURE 6   FIGURE 7   FIGURE 8

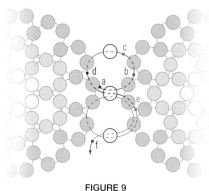

FIGURE 9

[7] Begin a third round off the second by picking up four 3mms, sewing through the 3mm your thread exited and the next two 3mms in the previous round (figure 6).

[8] Pick up three 3mms, and sew through the first 3mm in the previous stitch and the next three 3mms in the previous round (figure 7).

[9] Pick up three 3mms per stitch to complete the next nine stitches, continuing the alternating pattern of a ring with five 3mms and a ring with six 3mms. To complete the 10th stitch in the round, sew through the next 3mm in the first stitch of this round, pick up two 3mms, and sew through the next 3mm in the last stitch. Sew through the next two 3mms of the previous round and two 3mms in the first stitch of the third round (figure 8).

[10] Retrace the thread path to reinforce the rounds, and sew into the original ring, exiting next to the tail. Tie the ends together with a surgeon's knot, and sew through the next 3mm. Pull tight to hide the knot in the bead, and end the working thread and tail (Basics).

[11] Repeat steps 1–10 to make the second half of the pillow, then repeat two more times to complete the second set of halves for the other earring.

Joining the halves

[1] Add (Basics) a new 1-yd. (.9m) length of thread or Fireline to one of the halves, and exit an edge 3mm on a six-bead ring (figure 9, point a). Pick up a 3mm, and sew into the other half through an outer 3mm in a five-bead ring (a–b). Sew through the first 3mm in the next six-bead ring along the outer edge of the second half (b–c), pick up a 3mm, and sew through the

corresponding 3mm on the first half (c–d). Sew through the 3mm your thread exited, the first 3mm added, and the next 3mm in the ring of five on the second half (d–e).

[2] Continue, adding one bead per stitch (e–f), making six-bead rings around the circumference. You do not need to add any beads to complete the last stitch — simply sew through the existing six-bead ring of 3mms. Reinforce the connection round by sewing back through all of the stitches. End the thread.

[3] Repeat steps 1 and 2 with the remaining halves.

Earring assembly

[1] Cut two 4-in. (10cm) pieces of wire, and set one piece aside. Make a small plain loop (Basics) on one end of the wire.

[2] String a 3mm bead, a bead cap, a pillow, a bead cap, a 3mm bead, and a crimp bead (photo a).

[3] Using chainnose pliers, flatten the crimp bead (Basics) to hold the beads in place.

[4] Place a pencil or ¼-in. (6mm) dowel 1 in. (2.5cm) above the crimp bead, and bend the wire over it (photo b). Gently curve the wire after the bend. File the end of the wire.

[5] Repeat steps 1–4 with the remaining components to complete the second earring.

a   b

DESIGNER'S NOTE:
For thousands of years, mainland Chinese peoples have been creating some of the most sophisticated beadwork the world has known. Unfortunately for us, few of the designs have ever been published.

Although ancient Chinese bead-workers were skilled in bead embroidery, they achieved their greatest innovations in bead netting. They invented a number of two- and three-dimensional techniques that are, to this day, unknown outside of China.

The Chinese hexagonal pillow technique is one example. It is a recent addition to a set of hollow structures made entirely of beads and thread (or wire) that Chinese beadworkers began making in the last several centuries.

EDITOR'S NOTE:
Valerie used patina on all the sterling silver materials in this project, and used 3mm round beads to make the hexagonal pillows. You may also leave the sterling silver shiny, and 2mm beads will work in the place of the 3mms.

Double up

Daggers and crystals pair beautifully in figure-8 earrings

designed by **Gloria Farver**

MATERIALS

- **2** 16 x 5mm dagger beads
- **28** 3mm bicone crystals
- 2g size 15º Japanese seed beads
- pair of earring findings
- Fireline 6 lb. test
- beading needles, #12
- chainnose pliers

The workplace isn't always the easiest place to wear intricately embellished bracelets, which can interfere with the task at hand. Earrings, however, lend a little glamour to your workday without getting in the way.

stepbystep

[1] On 1 yd. (.9m) of Fireline, center two 15º seed beads, a repeating pattern of a 3mm bicone crystal and three 15ºs five times, a 3mm, and a 15º. Sew through the first 15º again, forming the bottom ring **(figure 1, a–b)**.

[2] Pick up a 15º, a repeating pattern of a 3mm and three 15ºs seven times, a 3mm, and a 15º. Sew through the first two 15ºs and 3mm in the bottom ring **(b–c)**.

[3] Pick up a 15º, and sew through the next 3mm in the bottom ring. Repeat, adding a 15º between each pair of 3mms in the bottom ring **(figure 2, a–b)**.

[4] Sew through the next 10 beads on the outer edge of the bottom ring **(b–c)**. Pick up three 15ºs, a dagger bead, and three 15ºs. Sew back through the 15º your thread just exited and the next 15º, 3mm, and two 15ºs on the outer edge of the bottom ring **(c–d)**. Secure the working thread in the beadwork with a few half-hitch knots (Basics), and trim.

[5] Thread a needle on the tail, and sew through the next 15º and 3mm in the top ring **(e–f)**. Pick up a 15º, and sew through the next 3mm in the top ring. Repeat around the ring **(f–g)**.

[6] Sew through the next 14 beads on the outer edge of the top ring **(g–h)**. Pick up 13 15ºs, and sew back through the 15º your thread just exited and the next four beads **(h–i)**. Secure the tail, and trim.

[7] Open the loop (Basics) of an earring finding, attach the dangle, and close the loop.

[8] Make a second earring.

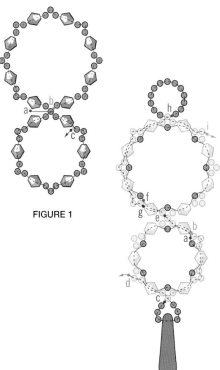

FIGURE 1

FIGURE 2

Make a Wish

Stitch up a dandy pair of flower-puff earrings

designed by **Tea Benduhn**

Arrange the fringe so the short stacks are in front of the tall stacks.

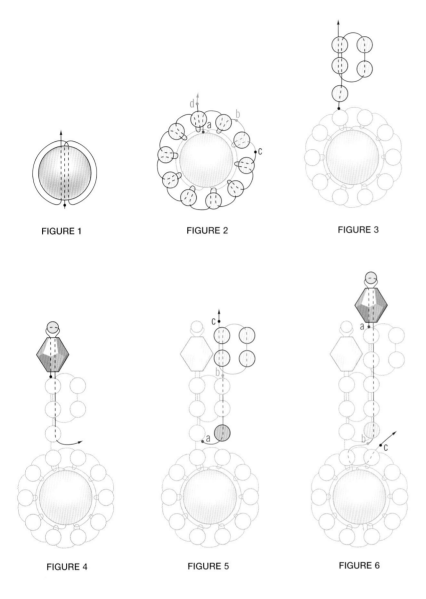

FIGURE 1

FIGURE 2

FIGURE 3

FIGURE 4

FIGURE 5

FIGURE 6

MATERIALS

- 2 6mm pearls
- 40 4mm bicone crystals
- 11º seed beads
  - 1–3g color A
  - 40 color B
- 1–3g 15º seed beads
- 2 5mm jump rings
- pair of earring findings
- Fireline 6 lb. test, or nylon beading thread, size D
- beading needles, #12
- 2 pairs of pliers

DESIGNER'S NOTE:

If you end up with more than 10 11ºs around the circumference of the pearl, adjust your count for crystals and color B 11º seed beads.

St. Petersburg chain makes a staggered fringe that mimics dandelion seeds just before you blow them away for the wind to carry your wish.

stepbystep

St. Petersburg fringe

[1] On 2 yd. (1.8 m) of Fireline or thread, pick up a 6mm pearl, leaving a 6-in. (15cm) tail. Sew through the 6mm twice in a figure-8 motion so the thread loops are on opposite sides **(figure 1)**.
[2] Pick up two color A 11º seed beads, and sew under a thread loop and back through the second A **(figure 2, a–b)**.
[3] Pick up an A, and sew under the thread loop and back up through the A

(b–c). Repeat to surround the 6mm, and when you reach the first A, sew through it, under the thread loop, and back through the A **(c–d)**.
[4] Working in St. Petersburg chain, pick up five As, and sew through the second and third As again so the fourth and fifth As form an adjacent column **(figure 3)**.
[5] Pick up a 4mm bicone crystal and a 15º seed bead, and sew back through the 4mm and the last three As in the column **(figure 4)**.

[6] Pick up a color B 11º seed bead, and sew through the two As in the next column **(figure 5, a–b)**.
[7] Pick up four As, and sew through the first two As just picked up again, sliding the four beads tight to the existing chain **(b–c)**.
[8] Pick up a 4mm and a 15º, and sew back through the 4mm, four As, and the B in the column **(figure 6, a–b)**.
[9] Sew down through the A your thread exited at the start of step 4, and sew up through the next A in the ring **(b–c)**.
[10] Repeat steps 4–9 around the 6mm, angling each new St. Petersburg fringe so the short stacks face the front of the earring.

Stem

[1] With your thread exiting an A in the ring, pick up two 15ºs, and sew down through the next A and up through the previous A **(figure 7)**.

[2] Repeat step 1 to attach another pair of 15ºs to the same pair of 11ºs, and sew up through the first 15º added.

[3] Using the four 15ºs just added as the base, work in tubular herringbone stitch (Basics) with 15ºs to make a stem that is 1 in. (2.5cm) long.

[4] To form a loop, work five flat herringbone stitches on one side of the tube by picking up two 15ºs, and sewing down through the next 15º and the first 15º just added. Step up through the top of a stack **(photo a)**.

[5] Sew the end of the five-stitch strip to the remaining stitch at the end of the tube **(photo b** and **figure 8)**. End the working thread and tail (Basics).

[6] Open a jump ring (Basics), and attach the herringbone loop and an earring finding.

[7] Make a second earring.

DESIGN ALTERNATIVE:
Instead of making a herringbone stem, string 1 in. (2.5cm) of 11ºs, 15ºs, or an alternating pattern of 11ºs and 15ºs. Pick up seven 15ºs and an earring finding, skip the last seven 15ºs, and sew back through the previous beads. Retrace the thread path, and end the thread.

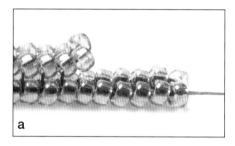

a

b

FIGURE 7

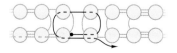

FIGURE 8

Woven royalty

Two-needle weaving produces a lovely lattice of seed beads and crystals

designed by **Melody MacDuffee**

Columns of crystals and seed beads stitch up easily, creating gorgeous earrings sure to make a statement at your next special event.

stepbystep

[1] Thread a needle on both ends of a 1-yd. (.9m) length of conditioned Nymo. Start a new length of thread for each row. With the first needle, pick up four 11º seed beads and a 4mm crystal, and slide the beads to the center of the thread. Using the second needle, pick up three 11ºs, and sew through the end 11º on the other side (figure 1).

[2] Pick up three 11ºs and one 4mm on each needle. Sew through the four 11ºs on that side and the three 11ºs just added on the other side. Repeat with the second needle (figure 2).

[3] Pick up a 4mm and cross the needles through it in opposite directions (figure 3). This completes one unit.

[4] Pick up three 11ºs with each needle, then cross the needles through a fourth 11º.

[5] Repeat steps 2–4 to complete five units.

[6] With one tail, pick up a soldered jump ring and sew through the end bead again. Repeat twice with the other tail.

[7] Sew through the beads to exit the first edge 4mm. Pick up a 3mm crystal and an 11º. Sew through the next edge 4mm. Continue adding a 3mm and an 11º between each 4mm along the edge. Repeat with the other thread on the other side. End both threads.

[8] Open the jump ring, attach it to the earring finding, and close the jump ring.

[9] Make a second earring.

MATERIALS

- bicone crystals
  - **36** 4mm
  - **20** 3mm
- 1g 11º Japanese seed beads
- **2** 3mm soldered jump rings
- pair of earring posts with ear nuts
- Nymo D conditioned with beeswax
- beading needles, #12

EDITOR'S NOTE:

Pull the inside thread slightly tighter than the outside thread when adding 3mm crystals to create a gentle curve.

FIGURE 1

FIGURE 2

FIGURE 3

Dutch treat

Make easy crystal earrings using the Dutch spiral technique

designed by **Cyndy Klein**

If you enjoy special-occasion jewelry, treat yourself to this pair of sparkling earrings. Worked in an easy variation of tubular peyote that yields the distinctive curves known as Dutch spiral, these earrings can be finished in an evening of leisurely beading.

FIGURE 1   FIGURE 2

stepbystep

[1] On 24 in. (61cm) of thread, string eight color A 11ºs, a 14º, two color B 11ºs, a heishi, a 4mm crystal, a heishi, two Bs, and a 14º. Go through the beads again to form a circle, leaving a 6-in. (15cm) tail. Tie the tail and working thread together with a surgeon's knot (Basics and **figure 1**).

[2] Work in peyote stitch (Basics): Go through the first A, pick up an A, skip the next A on the circle, and go through the third A. Repeat three times, going through the 14º to complete the last stitch **(figure 2, a–b)**. Keep the tension tight.

[3] Pick up a 14º, two Bs, a heishi, a 4mm crystal, a heishi, two Bs, and a 14º. (These are the floating beads.) Go through the first A added in step 2 **(b–c)**.

[4] Repeat steps 2–3 until you've used 11 4mm crystals. Finish with a four-bead peyote row of As, but don't end the thread.

[5] To make the dangle at the bottom of the earring, string a 14º, a 5mm crystal, and a 14º on a head pin. Trim the wire to ⅜ in. (1cm) above the end bead and make a small plain loop (Basics and **photo a**).

[6] Open the loop on the head pin and attach an eye pin. Close the loop **(photo b)**. Slide a heishi onto the eye pin, and insert the eye pin through the spiral between the first and second rows of floating beads. Exit between the last two rows **(photo c)**.

[7] Trim the wire to ⅜ in. above the spiral and make a loop as before. Open the loop, attach it to the earring finding, and close the loop **(photo d)**.

[8] To align the floating beads, use the thread from step 4 and sew back and forth through the 14ºs on the side of the spiral, working from end to end. Tighten the thread and secure the tails in the beadwork.

[9] Make a second earring.

MATERIALS

- bicone crystals
  - **22** 4mm
  - **2** 5mm
- **46** 4mm hex heishi or 4mm flat spacer beads
- seed beads
  - 3g 11º, in each of **2** colors: A, B
  - 2g 14º
- Power Pro 10 lb. or Fireline 6 lb. test
- beading needles, #12
- **2** 3-in. (7.6cm) eye pins
- **2** 2-in. (5cm) head pins
- pair of earring findings
- chainnose pliers
- roundnose pliers
- wire cutters

a

b

c

d

EDITOR'S NOTE:

The beadwork will feel flimsy as you stitch, but don't worry about the finished piece. Once you sew through the 14ºs in step 8, the tension changes considerably, and you'll have a firm, well-defined spiral.

STITCHING

Victorian
inspiration

Tiny gemstones and seed beads mimic the intricate, feminine style of the Victorian era in modified right-angle weave earrings

designed by **Anna Elizabeth Draeger**

DESIGNER'S NOTE:
Make a smaller version of these earrings by making only four picots in step 2, then adding 15º seed beads between those picots, as in step 3, and adding one 15º between the remaining 3mms in the ring. Add a small loop of seven 15ºs to the top 3mm in the ring for the earring finding.

Anna's aunt used to wear an antique pin that had layers of faceted garnets set in a circular pattern. That pin inspired Anna's love of gemstones, and though she's never found anything similar to that pin, it has influenced more than one of her designs. These earrings capture the Victorian look using faceted garnet beads.

stepbystep

[1] On 2 yd. (1.8 m) of Fireline, leaving a 6-in. (15cm) tail, pick up eight 3mm garnet beads. Sew through the first 3mm to form a ring (**figure 1, a–b**).
[2] Pick up four 3mms, skip the last three, and sew back through the first 3mm and the next 3mm in the ring (**b–c**), making the first picot. Repeat seven times to make a total of eight picots. Sew through the first 3mm in the ring (**c–d**) and on through four 3mms in the first picot (**d–e**).
[3] Pick up one 15º seed bead, and sew through the side 3mm in the next picot (**figure 2, a–b**). Pick up five 15ºs, and sew through the second 15º in the same direction (**b–c**). Pick up a 15º, and sew through the side 3mm from the previous picot, the next 15º, and the side 3mm in the next picot (**c–d**).
[4] Repeat step 3 seven times (**d–e**).
[5] Sew through the next two 3mms, a 15º, a 3mm from the next picot, and four 15ºs as shown (**figure 3, a–b**). Pick up a 3mm, a 15º, a 3mm, and seven 15ºs. Sew back through the first 15º of the seven to form a ring (**b–c**). Pick up a 3mm, a 15º, and a 3mm. Continue through four 15ºs and a side 3mm as shown (**c–d**).
[6] Secure the working thread with a few half-hitch knots (Basics), and trim. Repeat with the tail.
[7] Open the loop (Basics) of an earring finding, and attach the loop of 15ºs. Close the loops.
[8] Make a second earring.

MATERIALS
- **88** 3mm faceted round garnet beads
- **1g** 15º Japanese seed beads
- pair of earring findings
- Fireline 4 lb. test, smoke
- beading needles, #13
- **2** pairs of pliers

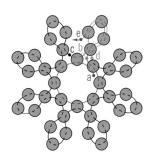

FIGURE 1

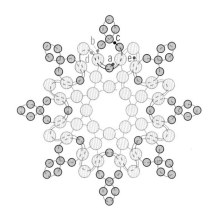

FIGURE 2

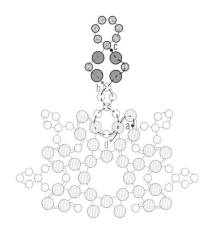

FIGURE 3

Spin clockwise or counterclockwise — it all depends on which way you stitch.

Spinner rims

Encircle a cabochon with complementary cubes

designed by **Virginia Jensen**

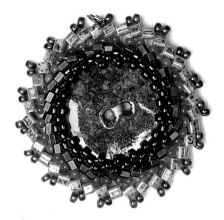

Any cabochons or sew-through buttons will work with this design — even an irregular shape, if the corners are soft and rounded. The beads on the inner edge of the circles are smaller than the beads on the outer edge, creating a natural curve.

stepbystep

Herringbone ring

[1] On 2 yd. (1.8m) of thread, attach a stop bead (Basics), leaving a 6-in. (15cm) tail. Pick up a 11º cylinder or hex-cut bead, a color A 15º seed bead, a 1.5mm cube bead, and a stop bead. Skip the stop bead, and sew back through the 1.5mm (**figure 1, a–b**).

[2] Pick up a 1.5mm, an A, and an 11º or hex-cut, and sew down through the previous 11º or hex-cut (**b–c**). Pick up a color B 15º seed bead, and sew back through the 11º or hex-cut just added (**c–d**).

[3] Pick up an 11º or hex-cut, an A, and a 1.5mm, and sew down through the previous 1.5mm (**d–e**). Pick up two color C 15º seed beads, and sew back through the 1.5mm just added (**e–f**).

[4] Repeat steps 2 and 3 until you have enough rows to fit around the circumference of your cabochon, ending with an even number of rows.

[5] With your thread exiting the last 11º or hex-cut added, sew through the 11º or hex-cut, A, and 1.5mm in the first row and the 1.5mm added in the last row (**figure 2, a–b**). Pick up a color C 15º, a 4mm soldered jump ring, and a C, and sew through the 1.5mm in row 1 (**b–c**). Sew through a few more rows, and tie a few half-hitch knots (Basics), but do not end the thread. Remove the stop beads from the tail by carefully pulling the thread out of the beads in row 1. If the beadwork comes loose at the join, snug up the beads with the tail. End the tail (Basics).

Bezel

[1] Tape or glue the cabochon or sew the button to the beading foundation. If using E6000 adhesive, allow the glue to dry for 15 minutes. Trim the foundation to about ⅛ in. (3mm) around the edge of the cabochon or button. If you are using Ultrasuede to cover the foundation, trace the foundation onto the Ultrasuede and trim. Set the Ultrasuede aside.

[2] Sew through the beadwork to exit an 11º or hex-cut. To stitch the beadwork to the foundation, center the beadwork around the cabochon or button, and sew through the foundation and the next cube (**photo a**, p. 56). Repeat around the beadwork.

MATERIALS

- **2** 12mm cabochons or flat-back crystals
- 1–2g 1.5mm cube beads
- 1–2g 11º cylinder or hex-cut beads
- 1–2g 15º seed beads in each of **3** colors: A, B, C
- **2** 4mm soldered jump rings
- pair of earring findings
- nylon beading thread, size D
- beading needles, #12
- double-sided tape or E6000 adhesive
- felt or Lacy's Stiff Stuff beading foundation
- Ultrasuede (optional)
- **2** pairs of pliers

EDITOR'S NOTES:

- If you are sewing a button to the beading foundation, you can tape or glue a piece of Ultrasuede to the back of the beading foundation to hide the button thread, and trim it to the same size as the foundation.
- Instead of attaching jump rings to the earrings, you can sew the earring findings to the beadwork.

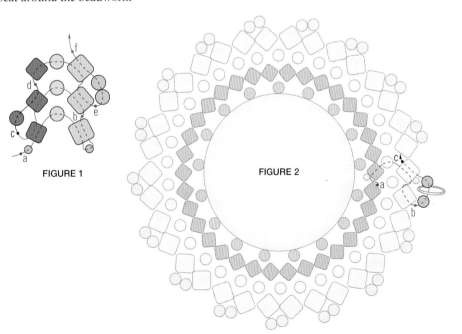

FIGURE 1

FIGURE 2

[3] Sew through the beadwork to exit a B. Pick up a B, and sew through the next B **(photo b)**. Repeat around the beadwork, and sew through the first B added.

[4] Pick up a B, skip the next B in the ring, and sew through the following B **(photo c)**. Continue working in tubular peyote stitch (Basics) to complete the round, and step up through the first B added **(photo d)**. If needed, work another round or two.

[5] If you are using Ultrasuede to cover the foundation, tape, glue, or whip stitch (Basics) the foundation to the Ultrasuede.

Assembly

[1] Sew through the beadwork to exit a pair of Cs. Pick up two Bs, and sew through the next pair of Cs **(figure 3)**. Repeat around the ring. End the thread.

[2] Open the loop of an earring finding (Basics), attach the 4mm soldered jump ring (Basics), and close the jump ring.

[3] Make a second earring.

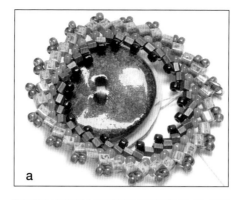

a

b

c

d

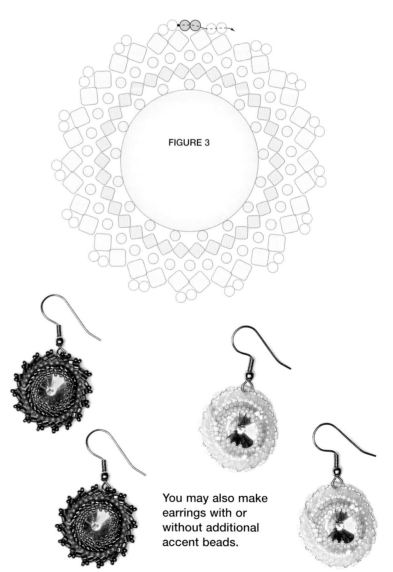

FIGURE 3

DESIGN NOTES:

• To make this project without sewing the beadwork to a foundation, stitch the herringbone ring around the cab, then tape or glue them both to a piece of plastic cut slightly smaller than the beadwork or about ¼ in. (6mm) larger than the cab.

• Using larger or smaller beads will change the dimensions of the curve. Use small beads for small cabs and large beads for large cabs.

You may also make earrings with or without additional accent beads.

Enchanted gazebo

Make beaded beads in monochromatic or complementary colors

designed by **Laura Landrum**

Construct open-air beaded beads with bugles, pearls, and crystals, and then string them with bead caps, rondelles, and pearls for a classy vintage look.

stepbystep

[1] Thread a needle on each end of 1½ yd. (1.4m) of Fireline, and center a 12mm twisted bugle bead.
[2] With each needle, pick up a 4mm pearl. With one needle, pick up a bugle, and cross the other needle through it (figure 1).
[3] Repeat step 2 until you have a total of five bugles (figure 2).
[4] With each needle, pick up a 4mm pearl, and cross both needles through the first bugle picked up in step 1 to form a ring.
[5] With each needle, pick up a 15º seed bead and a 4mm bicone crystal. With one needle, pick up a 15º, a 5 x 1.5mm

daisy spacer, and a 15º. Cross the other needle through the last three beads just picked up (figure 3, **a–b** and **aa–bb**).
[6] With each needle, pick up a 4mm bicone and a 15º, and cross both needles through the next bugle in the ring (**b–c** and **bb–cc**).
[7] Repeat steps 5 and 6 around the ring. With each needle, sew through the adjacent 4mm pearl.
[8] With one needle, pick up an 11º seed bead, and sew through the next 4mm pearl (figure 4, **a–b**). Repeat to add an 11º between all the 4mm pearls on this end of the ring (**b–c**). Repeat with the other needle on the other end of the ring, and end both threads (Basics).
[9] On a head pin, string: a 3mm round bead, a 7 x 4mm rondelle, an 8mm bead cap from inside to outside, a beaded bead, an 8mm bead cap from outside to inside, a rondelle, and a 3mm. Make a wrapped loop (Basics). Open the loop of an earring finding (Basics), and attach the wrapped loop.
[10] Make a second earring.

MATERIALS

- **10** 12mm twisted bugle beads
- **40** 4mm bicone crystals
- **20** 4mm crystal pearls
- **20** 11º seed beads
- **60** 15º seed beads
- **10** 5 x 1.5mm daisy spacers
- Fireline 6 lb. test
- beading needles, #10 or #12

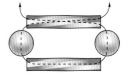

FIGURE 1

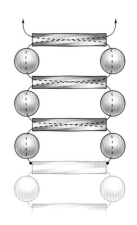

FIGURE 2

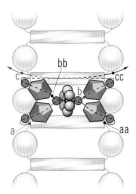

FIGURE 3

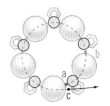

FIGURE 4

STITCHING

Fleurs de cristal

For a touch of glamour, use an easy weave to create little flower earrings

designed by **Katia Trebeau**

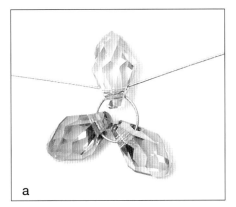

a

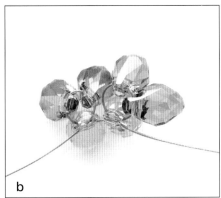

b

c

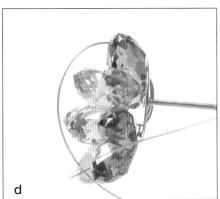

d

MATERIALS

- **24** 7 x 4mm crystal briolettes
- pair of 10mm padded post earring findings with holes
- Supplemax illusion cord, .010, or flexible beading wire, .010

EDITOR'S NOTES:

- Katia glued her earrings to the post for extra security, but you may find gluing yours unnecessary.
- If you can't get your briolettes as snug as you'd like them to be for your earring, sew through the outer ring of eight briolettes with your working thread and tie another knot before you start attaching the beads to the findings.

Simple rounds of tiny briolettes come together for petite blossoms with timeless appeal. These earrings work up so quickly, you'll soon have a garden of them.

stepbystep

[1] On 12 in. (30cm) of illusion cord or beading wire, pick up three briolettes, leaving a 6-in. (15cm) tail. Go through the first briolette again, forming a tight ring **(photo a)**.

[2] Pick up three briolettes, and go through the first briolette again, pulling the new ring tight against the first ring **(photo b)**. Repeat twice, for a total of four rings.

[3] Arrange the briolettes so that the four briolettes with the cords crossed through them are in the center, and the remaining eight briolettes fan out around them. Snug up the beads as much as possible **(photo c)**. Tie the working cord and tail together with a square knot (Basics).

[4] Go down through one hole of an earring post, and up through the other hole. Pull the cord over the top of the flower **(photo d)**. Tie the working cord and tail together with a square knot, pulling the cord down so it is nestled invisibly between the briolettes.

[5] Repeat step 4, but tie a knot with the working cord and tail before crossing over the beads, pulling both ends tight to hide under the beads.

[6] Repeat steps 4–5 until the earring is secure, taking care to pull the cord down under the briolettes, so it remains invisible. Finish with a surgeon's knot (Basics), and trim the ends under the beads.

[7] Make a second earring.

Mosaic
medallions

**Dangle tilework look-alikes
from your ears**

designed by **Liz Stahl**

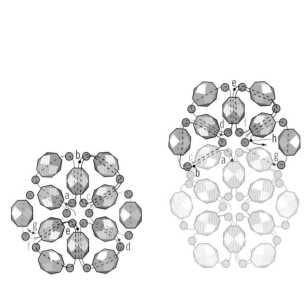

FIGURE 1

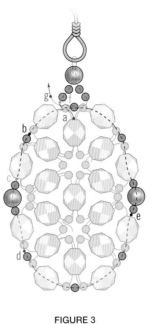

FIGURE 2   FIGURE 3

MATERIALS

- 4mm round fire-polished beads
  - **22** color A
  - **16** color B
- **6** 3mm glass pearls
- 1–2g 15º seed beads
- pair of earring findings
- Fireline 6 lb. test
- beading needles, #12

Use modified right-angle weave to work up a quick pair of earrings with a center of sweet fire-polished bead flowers and an edging in a complementary or contrasting color.

stepbystep

Medallions

Lower medallion

[1] On 26 in. (66cm) of Fireline, leave an 8-in. (20cm) tail and pick up a repeating pattern of a 15º seed bead and a color A 4mm fire-polished bead three times. Sew through all six beads again to form a ring. Tie a square knot (Basics), and sew through the next two beads to exit an A (figure 1, a–b).
[2] Pick up a 15º, an A, a 15º, an A, and a 15º, and sew through the A your thread exited at the start of this step and the first four beads just added (b–c).
[3] Pick up a 15º, an A, a 15º, a color B 4mm fire-polished bead, and a 15º, and sew through the A your thread exited at the start of this step and the first two beads just added (c–d).
[4] Pick up a 15º, a B, a 15º, an A, and a 15º, and sew through the A your thread exited at the start of this step and the first four beads just added (d–e).
[5] Repeat step 3 (e–f).
[6] Join the ends to form a ring: Pick up a 15º, a B, and a 15º, and sew through the adjacent A from step 1.

Pick up a 15º, and sew through the A your thread exited at the start of the step (f–g).
[7] Sew through the beadwork to exit the inside A between the two As on the outer edge (figure 2, point a). With the tail, sew through the center ring of 15º's. End the tail (Basics).

Upper medallion

[1] Sew through the next 15º and A along the outer edge (a–b).
[2] Pick up a 15º, a B, a 15º, an A, and a 15º, and sew through the A your thread exited at the start of this step (b–c) and the first four beads just added (c–d).
[3] Pick up a 15º, an A, a 15º, a B, and a 15º. Sew through the A your thread exited at the start of this step and the first two beads just added (d–e).
[4] Repeat step 2 (e–f).
[5] Pick up a 15º, and sew through the adjacent A in the lower medallion (f–g). Pick up a 15º, a B, and a 15º, and sew through the A your thread exited at the start of this step (g–h). Sew through all six 15º's in the center ring, and snug up the beads.

DESIGN NOTE:

Substitute 4mm bicone crystals for the color B fire-polished beads to add even more glamour.

Edging

[1] Sew through the beadwork to exit the top inside A in the upper medallion (figure 3, point a). Sew through the next 15º, B, and 15º along the outer edge (a–b). Pick up a 15º, and sew through the next 15º and B (b–c).
[2] Pick up a 15º, a 3mm pearl, and a 15º, and sew through the following B and 15º along the outer edge (c–d).
[3] Pick up a 15º, and sew through the next 15º, B, and 15º. Repeat this stitch twice, but in the last repeat, sew through only a 15º and a B (d–e).
[4] Repeat step 2, then pick up a 15º, and sew through the next 15º, B, and 15º. Pick up a 15º, and sew through the next 15º (e–f).
[5] Pick up two 15º's, a 3mm, and an earring finding, and sew back through the 3mm. Pick up two 15º's, and sew through the three 15º's your thread exited at the start of this step (f–g). Retrace the thread path of the earring connection, and end the thread.
[6] Make a second earring.

Love thy lobes

Hearts and teardrops dangle from a crystal strand adorned with seed bead fringe

designed by **Anna Elizabeth Draeger**

For adorable earrings that will please at Valentine's Day and year round, stitch up these simple fringed patterns. Make your own heart-shaped earring wires for an extra special touch.

stepbystep

Long earrings

[1] On a 1-yd. (.9m) length of thread, pick up eight 15º seed beads, a 12mm heart crystal, eight 15ºs, a 4mm bicone crystal, a 15º, a 4mm round crystal, a 15º, a 6mm round crystal, a 15º, a 4mm round, a 15º, a 4mm bicone, and a 15º. Center the beads on the thread (figure 1, a–b).

[2] Pick up a soldered jump ring, and sew back through the beads, continuing through the first eight 15ºs strung in step 1 (b–c).

[3] Pick up seven 15ºs, skip the last 15º, and sew back through the next two 15ºs (c–d).

[4] Pick up three 15ºs, skip the last 15º, sew back through the next two 15ºs, and continue through the next two 15ºs of the original seven (d–e).

[5] Repeat step 4 twice, going through the next two 15ºs on the bail the second time (e–f).

[6] Repeat steps 3–5 to complete three more sets of fringe, exiting the last 15º on the bail (f–g). Secure the thread with half-hitch knots (Basics) between a few beads.

[7] Thread a needle on the tail, and sew through the eight 15ºs on the other side of the bail. Work the fringe on this side of the heart, as in steps 3–6.

[8] Make a second earring to match the first.

Short earrings

[1] On 1 yd. (.9m) of thread, pick up four 15º seed beads, an 8mm heart crystal, and four 15ºs. Then pick up a 4mm bicone crystal and a 15º three times (figure 2, a–b). Center the beads on the thread.

[2] Pick up a soldered jump ring, and sew back through the beads to point c.

[3] Pick up five 15ºs, skip the last 15º, and sew back through the next three 15ºs (c–d).

[4] Pick up four 15ºs, skip the last 15º, and sew through the next three 15ºs.

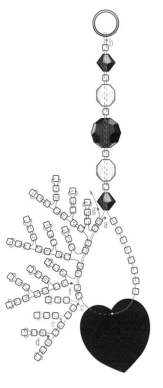

FIGURE 1

FIGURE 2

EDITOR'S NOTE:
Vary the length of the fringe to suit the size of your drop bead.

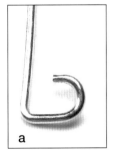

a

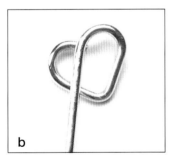

b

c

Continue through the next 15º of the original five and through the next 15º on the bail (d–e).

[5] Repeat steps 3 and 4 to complete three more sets of fringe (e–f). Secure the tail with half-hitch knots (Basics), and trim.

[6] Thread a needle on the tail, and sew through the four 15ºs on the other side of the bail. Repeat steps 3–5.

[7] Make a second earring to match the first.

Heart earring wires

[1] Cut a 4-in. (10cm) piece of wire, and make a right-angle bend ⅜ in. (1cm) from the end of a 4-in. (10cm) length of wire.

[2] Position your roundnose pliers at the very tip of the wire, and make a curve (photo a).

[3] Position the roundnose pliers about ¼ in. (6mm) from the bend on the long end of the wire. Bend the wire around the pliers to mirror the other side (photo b).

[4] Bend the long wire back on itself (photo c).

[5] String a 4mm bicone crystal, and form the remaining wire around a ¼ in. (6mm) dowel to make the curve. Trim the wire to the desired length, and file the end.

[6] To attach an earring dangle, open the end of the heart shape as you would a loop (Basics), slide the soldered jump ring in, and close the heart.

MATERIALS

both earring projects
- Silamide or Nymo D conditioned with beeswax
- beading needles, #13

long earrings
- 2 12mm heart crystals
- 2 6mm round crystals
- 4 4mm round crystals
- 4 4mm bicone crystals
- 2g 15º Japanese seed beads
- 2 3mm soldered jump rings

short earrings
- 2 8mm heart crystals
- 6 4mm bicone crystals
- 2g 15º Japanese seed beads
- 2 3mm soldered jump rings

pair of heart-shaped earring wires
- 2 4mm bicone crystals
- 8 in. (20cm) 22-gauge wire
- chainnose pliers
- roundnose pliers
- wire cutters
- ¼-in. (6mm) dowel
- metal file

Rivoli dangles

Stitch delicate crystal bezels for brilliant rivolis

designed by **Gail Damm**

MATERIALS

- 2 14mm Swarovski rivolis
- 62 3mm bicone crystals
- 3g 15º seed beads
- 2 two-to-one connectors
- 3½ in. (8.9cm) chain, 2–4mm links
- 8 3–4mm inside-diameter jump rings
- pair of earring findings
- Fireline 6 lb. test
- beading needles, #12
- bentnose pliers
- chainnose pliers
- wire cutters

Trendy Swarovski rivolis meet vintage-style findings in these colorful earrings. Chain and two-to-one connectors add swing to the sparkle.

stepbystep

[1] On a comfortable length of Fireline, attach a stop bead (Basics), leaving a 6-in. (15cm) tail. Pick up a 3mm bicone crystal and four 15º seed beads. Sew through the first 15º again, making a picot **(figure 1, a–b)**. Repeat nine times, and sew through the first 3mm and three 15ºs to form a ring **(b–c)**.
[2] Pick up three 15ºs, and sew through the 15º your thread exited at the start of this step and the first two 15ºs just picked up **(c–d)**.
[3] Pick up an alternating pattern of a 3mm and a 15º nine times. Pick up a 3mm, and sew through the 15º your thread exited at the start of this step and

the first 3mm and 15º just picked up to form a ring **(d–e)**.
[4] Pick up a 15º, sew through the point 15º of the next picot on the first ring, pick up a 15º, and sew through the 15º your thread exited at the start of this step and the next 3mm and 15º **(e–f)**. Fold the rings together, and repeat around, sandwiching the rivoli between the two rings after two or three stitches. Exit the center bead of the first join **(figure 2, point a)**.
[5] Pick up a 15º, a 3mm, and a 15º, and sew through the next center 15º **(a–b)**. Repeat around the ring.
[6] Sew through the beadwork to exit a 3mm on the back of the rivoli **(figure 3, point a)**. Pick up five 15ºs, sew through

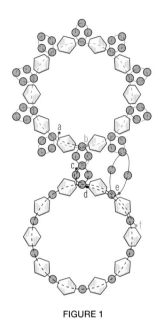

FIGURE 1

FIGURE 2

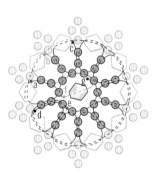

FIGURE 3

a

b

the 3mm again, and continue through the next 15ºs and 3mm in the ring (a–b).

[7] Pick up three 15ºs, sew through the first two 15ºs of the previous loop, the 3mm your thread exited at the start of this step, and the next 15º and 3mm in the ring (b–c). Repeat seven times (c–d).

[8] Sew through the next two 15ºs of the first loop, pick up a 15º, sew through the last two 15ºs of the last loop, and continue through the next 3mm and three 15ºs of the loop (d–e). Sew through all the center 15ºs of the loops (e–f).

[9] Pick up a 3mm, skip five 15ºs in the inner ring, and sew through the next 15º (f–g). Retrace the thread path through the crystal, secure the working thread and tail with a few half-hitch knots (Basics), and trim.

[10] Cut two ¾-in. (1.9cm) pieces of chain. Open a jump ring (Basics), slide it between the rivoli and a seed bead in the outer ring, attach the end link of a chain, and close the jump ring (photo a).

[11] Open a jump ring, attach the other end link of the chain and a loop of a two-to-one connector, and close the jump ring. Open another jump ring, attach the end link of the second chain and the other loop of the connector, and close the jump ring.

[12] Decide where to attach the second chain to the rivoli so it will hang evenly. Open a fourth jump ring, attach the end link of the chain and the outer ring of crystals, and close the jump ring (photo b).

[13] Open the loop of an earring finding, attach the top loop of the connector, and close the loop.

[14] Make a second earring.

EDITOR'S NOTE:

Gail used 15º Japanese seed beads for her earrings, but 15º Charlottes will also work. If you use Charlottes, however, leave a little slack in the two rings as you stitch the bezel. If the rings are too tight, it's difficult to fit them around the rivoli. You can use the starting tail and working thread to tighten the rings after the rivoli is in place, if necessary.

Floral filigree

Fine wirework makes tiny blooming vines

designed by **Melody MacDuffee**

MATERIALS

- **44** 2–3mm faceted gemstone rondelles, color A
- **16** 2–3mm smooth round gemstone beads, color A
- **44** 2–3mm smooth round gemstone beads, color B
- 14 in. (36cm) 20-gauge wire, half-hard
- 15 ft. (4.6m) 28-gauge wire, dead-soft
- 6 in. (15cm) cable chain, 1.25mm links
- pair of earring findings
- chainnose pliers
- roundnose pliers
- wire cutters

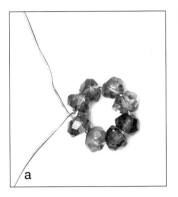
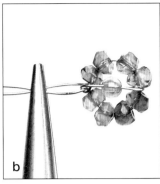
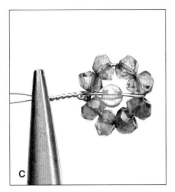

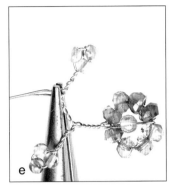
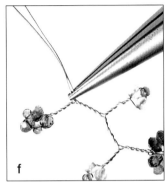
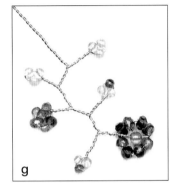
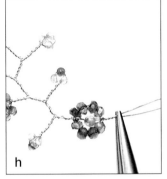

For Melody, making floral wire filigree is like cultivating a colorful little garden and nudging it into bloom. With gemstones for the flowers, these coiled, shaped, and twisted wire earrings combine several of her favorite things in one project.

FIGURE 1

stepbystep

Filigree

[1] To begin the central flower of the filigree, center eight color A rondelles on 1 ft. (30cm) of 28-gauge wire. Cross one end of the wire over the other and wrap tightly once or twice, forming a ring (photo a).

[2] Cross one wire over the ring, passing the wire between the middle two beads on the opposite side. String a color B gemstone on the wire, cross back to the other side so that the B rests in the center of the ring, and twist the wire ends once or twice.

[3] Hold the wire ends slightly apart, with either the thumb and forefinger of your nondominant hand or chainnose pliers, approximately ¼ in. (6mm) from the beadwork (photo b). Grasp the beadwork with your dominant hand, and twist it a few times (photo c).

Note: The wire should be securely twisted, but not too tight. Too little twist will result in flimsy-looking filigree. Too much twist may result in brittle wire that breaks easily. If it looks like one wire end is twisted around the other, you probably weren't holding the two ends slightly apart before you began twisting.

[4] On one wire end, string a B, a round color A gemstone, and a B. Holding the wire ends ⅜ in. (1cm) from the main stem, twist them together at the base of the beads, forming a ring. Holding the two wire ends slightly apart at the point where the branch meets the main stem, twist the branch a few times (photo d).

[5] Repeat steps 3 and 4 on the other side of the main stem (photo e).

[6] On the first side of the main stem, repeat steps 3 and 4, substituting an A rondelle, an A round, an A rondelle, an A round, and an A rondelle for the B, A, and B (photo f).

[7] Continuing on the same side of the main stem, repeat steps 3 and 4, substituting three Bs for the B, A, and B.

Repeat this step on the other side of the main stem to make a final branch. Twist an additional 1 in. (2.5cm) of main stem and trim the excess (photo g).

[8] Center a 10-in. (25cm) piece of 28-gauge wire in the flower made in steps 1 and 2, positioning it opposite the original stem. Wrap each half of the wire around the base wire, pulling the ends tight to secure them. Twist the wires for ¼ in. (6mm) (photo h).

[9] Repeat steps 4–7, making a mirror image of the first side (photo i).

[10] Repeat steps 1–9 for the other earring, making it match the first.

Frames

[1] Cut a 2¼-in. (5.7cm) piece of 20-gauge wire. Using **figure 1** as a template, bend the wire in half, against its natural curve, to make a slightly curved V, and make a simple loop at each end (Basics).

[2] Cut a 4½-in. (11.4cm) piece of 20-gauge wire, and, using **figure 2** as a

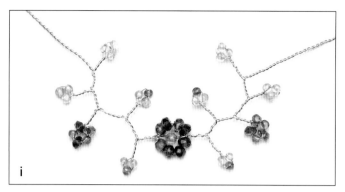

i

j

k

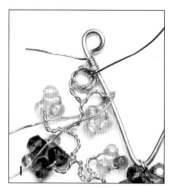

l

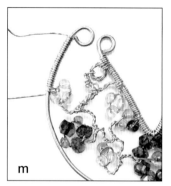

m

n

o

FIGURE 2

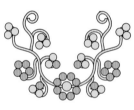

FIGURE 3

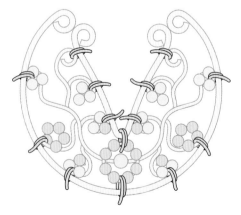

FIGURE 4

template, gently bend the wire into a U, following its natural curve. Make a simple loop at each end.

[3] With roundnose pliers, and using **figure 3** as a guide, gently curve a piece of filigree **(photo j)** to fit around the V-shaped frame and within the U-shaped frame.

[4] Using scrap wire, temporarily tack the filigree to the inner frame **(photo k)** at the points of contact shown in **figure 4**. Your points of contact may differ from those shown here — what's important is that your filigree lies comfortably and attractively between the frames.

[5] Cut a 2-ft. (61cm) piece of 28-gauge wire, and, leaving a ½–1-in. (1.3–2.5cm) tail, wrap it around the inner frame two or three times just below one of the loops.

[6] Wrap the wire tightly and evenly around the frame until you reach the first contact point. Push the coils together as needed to cover the frame completely. Remove the tacking wire, and continue coiling, going through the filigree one or more times at the contact point **(photo l)**.

[7] Continue coiling the working wire around the frame, removing the tacking wires as you go, until the filigree is

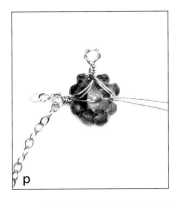

p

q

r

s

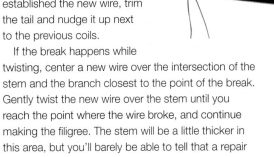

EDITOR'S NOTE:

If your wire breaks as you are twisting or coiling it, don't despair — you may be able to save your work. If the break happens while coiling, just cut it off at the break, begin a new piece of wire right after the break, and continue coiling. Once you've established the new wire, trim the tail and nudge it up next to the previous coils.

If the break happens while twisting, center a new wire over the intersection of the stem and the branch closest to the point of the break. Gently twist the new wire over the stem until you reach the point where the wire broke, and continue making the filigree. The stem will be a little thicker in this area, but you'll barely be able to tell that a repair was made.

anchored to the frame and you reach the other loop on the frame. Trim the tails.

[8] Repeat steps 4–7 to attach the filigree to the outer frame (photo m). You may find that you do not need to tack the filigree in place once you get the hang of coiling. You'll just need to check often to make sure you haven't passed a contact point. Also, as you near the end, you may find that you have more frame wire than you need. If that's the case, simply snip off the extra wire and re-form the loop.

[9] Repeat steps 1–8 to make second earring.

Assembly

[1] Cut two three-link pieces and two 12-link pieces of chain.

[2] With a 10-in. (25cm) piece of 28-gauge wire, repeat steps 1–3 of filigree.

[3] With the front of the flower facing forward, and working with the two wire ends as though they were one, make the first half of a wrapped loop (Basics). String an end link of one three-link and one 12-link chain into the wrapped loop, making sure the three-link chain is on the outer edge (photo n). Finish the wraps.

[4] Guide the wires behind the next two beads of the flower, establishing the top

of the flower. Wrap each wire between the middle two top beads from front to back, pulling tightly (photo o).

[5] Twist an 1/8-in. (3mm) length of stem, and make a wrapped loop. Guide the wires behind the next two beads and wrap them around the wire base (photo p).

[6] Twist an 1/8-in. (3mm) length of stem, and make the first half of a wrapped loop. String an end link of each remaining chain into the loop, making sure the three-link piece is on the outer edge. Finish the wraps (photo q).

[7] Making sure the filigree and the flower you just made are facing the same way, open an outer frame loop (Basics), and attach the remaining end link of the corresponding three-link chain. Close the loop. Repeat with the other loop and three-link chain (photo r).

[8] Cross the 12-link chains, and attach each remaining end link to the corresponding loop of the inner frame (photo s).

[9] Open the loop of an earring finding, and attach the earring. Close the loop.

[10] Repeat steps 1–9 for the other earring.

Dotty dangles

Petite buttons dance on easy layered earrings

designed by **Lesley Weiss**

These tiny shank buttons reminded Lesley of polka dots, perfect for a pair of light, summery earrings. Using two shades of seed beads adds dimension and movement to the dangles. Lesley chose shimmering pastels, but these earrings would be just as fun in bold, bright colors.

MATERIALS

- **10** 6mm shank buttons
- 2g 8º seed beads in each of **2** colors: A, B
- **12** 7mm inside-diameter (ID) 18-gauge jump rings
- **2** 3mm ID 20-gauge jump rings
- pair of earring findings
- **2** pairs of chainnose pliers

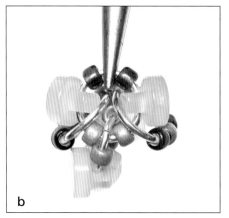

a

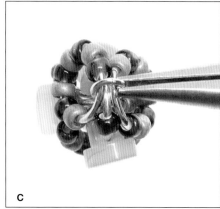

b

c

stepbystep

[1] Open five of the 7mm jump rings (Basics). On each of two jump rings, string an alternating pattern of a color A 8º seed bead and a color B 8º seed bead three times. Close the jump rings. On each of two jump rings, string an alternating pattern of an A and a B four times, and close the jump rings. On the fifth jump ring, string an alternating pattern of an A and a 6mm button three times, then string an A, and close the jump ring **(photo a)**.

[2] Open a 7mm jump ring, and string a B, a button, a six-bead jump ring, an A, the jump ring with three buttons, an A, a six-bead jump ring, a button, and a B. Close the jump ring **(photo b)**.

[3] Open a 3mm jump ring, and attach an eight-bead jump ring, the two-button jump ring from step 2, and an eight-

bead jump ring. Close the jump ring **(photo c)**.

[4] Open the loop of an earring finding, attach the 3mm jump ring, and close the loop.

[5] Make a second earring.

Pearl
on a wire

Enjoy the subtle glow of pearls perched in a simple wire frame

designed by **Melanie Hazen**

This quick-and-easy project allows you to create a fun pair of earrings, and maybe a matching pendant or ring, using miscellaneous beads in your stash.

stepbystep

[1] Cut a 2½-in. (6.4cm) piece of wire.

[2] Make a plain loop (Basics) at each end of the wire.

[3] Shape the wire around the dowel or the ring mandrel at the size 1½ mark **(photo a)**. Slide the wire off dowel or the mandrel.

[4] Using chainnose pliers, bend the loops so that they are parallel to each other **(photo b)**.

[5] On a head pin, string a 3mm silver bead, one of the wire loops, a pearl, the other wire loop, and a 3mm.

[6] Holding the beads tight against the head pin, make a right-angle bend in the head pin against the last 3mm, toward the center of the wire circle **(photo c)**.

[7] Use chainnose pliers to tightly wrap the head pin tail around the wire circle several times. Trim the wire tail as close to the wraps as possible, and press it against the circle **(photo d)**.

[8] Open the loop (Basics) of an earring finding, attach the wire circle, and close the loop.

[9] Make a second earring.

a

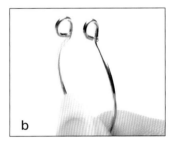

b

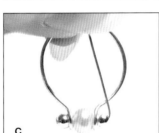

c

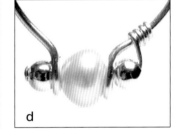

d

MATERIALS

- 2 5mm button pearls
- 4 3mm round silver beads
- 5 in. (13cm) 20-gauge sterling silver wire, dead-soft
- 2 2-in. (5cm) 24-gauge silver head pins
- pair of earring findings
- ring mandrel or ½-in. (1.3cm) dowel
- chainnose pliers
- roundnose pliers
- wire cutters

DESIGNER'S NOTE:

To make a matching pendant, increase the length and gauge of the wire, and use larger beads.

EDITOR'S NOTES:

- If you don't have a ring mandrel or a ½-in. (1.3cm) dowel, any sturdy round tube with the correct diameter can be used.
- You can make a unique ring using this design. Use a heavier gauge wire, form it to the correct size for your finger, and omit the earring finding.

Swinging crystals

Wirework and crystals make large yet light earrings

designed by **Melody MacDuffee**

MATERIALS

- bicone crystals
  - **2** 8mm, color A
  - **2** 6mm, color B
  - **32** 4mm, color A
  - **24** 4mm, color B
- 3mm fire-polished beads
  - **46** color C (to match color A)
  - **22** color D (to match color B)
  - **34** color E (accent color)
- 11º seed or cylinder beads (all to match color A)
  - **5g** color F, matte
  - **5g** color G, metallic
  - **5g** color H, transparent or silver-lined
- 13 in. (33cm) 22-gauge sterling silver wire, half-hard
- 4 yd. (3.7m) 28-gauge sterling silver wire, dead-soft
- **2** 2-in (5cm) sterling silver head pins
- **2** 4–6mm soldered jump rings
- pair of earring findings
- chainnose pliers
- roundnose pliers
- wire cutters

Build loops upon loops of monochromatic crystals and beads for flashy earrings. You can also try one as a pendant!

stepbystep

When complete, these earrings have a distinct front and back. To help you identify the front while you're working, bend the end loops of the U-shaped base so the openings face toward the back. This will also give the finished earrings a cleaner look.

Outer round

[1] Cut two 6½-in. (16.5cm) pieces of wire. Set one piece aside for the second earring. Use roundnose pliers to form a loop on each end of the wire. Gently bend the wire into a U, making sure that both loops face the same direction (**photo a**).

[2] Cut a 1-yd. (.9m) piece of 28-gauge wire. Secure the wire by wrapping it tightly four or five times around the left side

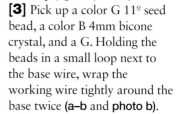

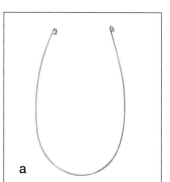

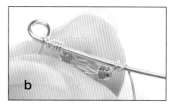

of the U-shaped base, next to the loop (**figure, point a**).

[3] Pick up a color G 11º seed bead, a color B 4mm bicone crystal, and a G. Holding the beads in a small loop next to the base wire, wrap the working wire tightly around the base twice (**a–b** and **photo b**).

[4] Pick up a color F 11º, a color A 4mm bicone, and an F, and wrap the working wire around the base twice as before (**b–c**).

[5] Repeat steps 3 and 4 until you have 23 beaded loops around the outside of the base and have reached the end loop

a

b

on the right side. Wrap the wire tightly around the base four or five times to match the other end (c–d). Do not trim.

Inner round 1

[1] Continuing with the 28-gauge wire, pick up a color H 11º, a 3mm color C fire-polished bead, and an H. Wrap once around the base, aligning the loop of crystals with the corresponding loop on the outer round (d–e and **photo c**).
[2] Pick up a G, a C, and a G, and wrap the wire around the base as before (e–f).
[3] Repeat steps 1 and 2 until you have completed 23 inner loops that line up with the outer loops (f–g). Tightly wrap the wire around the base several times to secure it at **point g**, and trim.

Inner round 2

[1] Cut 1 ft. (30cm) of 28-gauge wire. Secure the end with two or three wraps on the third inner loop, at **point h**.
[2] Pick up an H, a color E fire-polished bead, and an H. With the working wire, go through the next loop of the first inner round, front to back, positioning the wire between the C and lower G. Squeeze the working wire at that point to establish the new loop (h–i and **photo d**).
[3] Repeat step 2 until you have 17 loops total (i–j). Wrap tightly at **point j** two or three times, and trim.

Inner round 3

[1] Cut 1 ft. (30cm) of 28-gauge wire. Secure the end at **point k** with two or three wraps as before.
[2] Pick up an F, a G, a color D fire-polished bead, a G, and an F. Secure the working wire to the previous round, as in step 2 of "Inner round 2" (k–l).

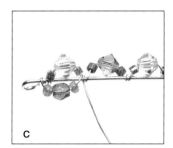

c

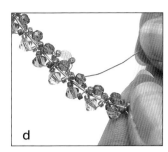

d

Outer Round

Inner Round 1

Inner Round 2

Inner Round 3

Inner Round 4

a g
b
c
h
i
k
n
o

d
e
f
j
m
p

FIGURE

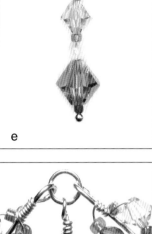

e

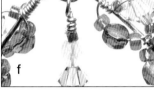

f

[3] Repeat step 2 to form a total of 11 loops (l–m). Wrap tightly at **point m** two or three times, and trim.

Inner round 4

[1] Cut 6 in. (15cm) of 28-gauge wire. Secure the end at **point n** with two or three wraps.
[2] Pick up an H, an A, and an H, and secure the working wire as before (n–o). Repeat three times for a total of four evenly spaced loops at the bottom

center of the base (o–p). Secure the end at **point p** with two or three wraps, and trim.

Assembly

[1] On a head pin, pick up an F, an 8mm bicone, an E, a G, a 6mm bicone, a G, an E, an A, an E, and an H. Make the first half of a wrapped loop (Basics and **photo e**). Attach the loop to a soldered jump ring, and finish the wraps.

EDITOR'S NOTE:

If you're having trouble fitting all 23 loops on the outer round of the base wire, gently slide the existing loops along the wire to make room for the last few wraps.

[2] Open one loop of the base, attach the soldered jump ring, and close the loop. Repeat with the other loop, making sure the dangle hangs in the middle (**photo f**).
[3] Open the loop of an earring finding, attach the earring, and close the loop.
[4] Make a second earring.

WIREWORK & CHAIN MAIL

Geometric style

For a contemporary look, pair cube crystals with square jump rings and custom findings

designed by **Anna Elizabeth Draeger**

MATERIALS

- **6** 6mm cube crystals with offset holes, Swarovski 5600
- 10 in. (25cm) 22-gauge wire, half-hard
- **2** 1-in. (2.5cm) 22-gauge head pins
- **4** 6mm square soldered jump rings
- ¼-in. (6mm) pen or dowel
- chainnose pliers
- flatnose pliers
- roundnose pliers
- wire cutters

FIGURE

stepbystep

[1] Cut a 1-in. (2.5cm) piece of 20-gauge wire. Make a plain loop (Basics) on one end. String a crystal. Make a plain loop above the crystal in the same plane as the first **(photo)**. Repeat to make a total of six crystal units.

[2] Cut a 3-in. (7.6cm) piece of 22-gauge wire.

[3] Make a right-angle bend ¼ in. (6mm) from the end of the wire. Referring to the figure, make two more right-angle bends to form a diamond shape. After you make the diamond shape, wrap the wire around a pen or dowel to curve the center **(figure)**. Use flatnose pliers to bend the end of the wire away from the loop, as in the figure.

[4] Open one loop of a crystal unit (Basics), and attach the earring wire. Close the loop. Open the other loop on the crystal unit, and attach a soldered jump ring. Close the loop. Connect another crystal unit and jump ring. End by connecting the head pin unit.

[5] Make a second earring.

Twisted sisters

A few wire techniques and a handful of materials produce a pair of earrings in minutes

designed by **Kimberly Berlin**

Use smaller beads and 22-gauge wire to make a dainty version of these earrings.

 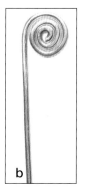  

a   b   c   d

Wrap wire around a few spare beads for a sophisticated twist on the traditional drop earring. Mix wood, gemstone, and crystals for a natural feel, or go glam with all crystals.

MATERIALS

- wood, gemstone, glass, crystal, or pearl beads
  - 2 14mm
  - 2 10mm
  - 2 8mm
- 2 4mm flat spacers
- 12 in. (30cm) 18-gauge wire
- 2 3-in. (7.6cm) 24-gauge head pins
- pair of earring findings
- chainnose pliers
- flatnose pliers
- roundnose pliers
- wire cutters

stepbystep

[1] On a 3-in. (7.6cm) head pin, string a 4mm spacer, a 14mm bead, a 10mm bead, and an 8mm bead. Make a wrapped loop (Basics and **photo a**).
[2] Cut a 6-in. (15cm) piece of 18-gauge wire. On one end, make a small loop with the tip of your round-nose pliers. Hold the loop with your flatnose pliers, and wrap the wire around the loop three times to create a flat spiral (**photo b**).
[3] Hold the spiral against the 14mm bead, and wrap the wire once around the spot where the 14mm and the 10mm beads meet (**photo c**).
[4] Continue wrapping the wire around the 10mm, the spot where the 10mm meets the 8mm, and the 8mm.

[5] Wrap the wire twice around the wraps of the wrapped loop, and trim the excess wire (**photo d**).
[6] Open the loop (Basics) of an earring finding, and attach the wrapped loop.
[7] Make the second earring as a mirror image of the first.

Night on the town

Dress up your ears with classy chandeliers

designed by
Rachel Nelson-Smith

MATERIALS

- **4** 6 x 9mm or 5 x 7mm teardrops, color A
- **2** 8mm round beads, color B
- **4** 6mm round beads or 8mm rondelles, color B
- 3mm beads
  - **44** color A
  - **22** color B
  - **24–26** color C
- **8** 3mm spacers
- **14 in.** (36cm) 18-gauge wire
- **13 ft.** (4m) 24-gauge wire
- pair of earring findings
- chainnose pliers
- roundnose pliers
- wire cutters

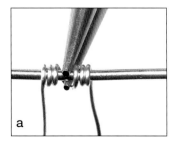

a

Dangle a variety of beads from wire loops to make a pair of fun, fringy earrings. Combine crystals, fire-polished beads, pearls, and gemstones for maximum impact.

stepbystep

Getting started

[1] Cut a 6-in. (15cm) piece of 18-gauge wire and a 1-ft. (30cm) piece of 24-gauge wire.

[2] Make a bend ½ in. (1.3cm) from one end of the 24-gauge wire, and place the 18-gauge wire against the bend. Wrap the 24-gauge wire around the 18-gauge wire three times.

[3] With the tips of your roundnose pliers, grasp the 18-gauge wire next to the wraps you just made. Go under the lower jaw of the pliers with the 24-gauge wire, and wrap it around the 18-gauge piece three times **(photo a)**.

[4] Repeat step 3 eight times to make a total of nine loops. Trim the excess wire.

[5] Center the nine-loop segment on the 18-gauge wire, and bend the wire into a teardrop shape, with the ends crossing about ¾ in. (1.9cm) from the top **(photo b)**.

[6] Where the wires cross, bend one end straight up, then use roundnose pliers to bend it into a loop **(photo c)**.

[7] Wrap the other wire around the first. Trim the excess wire **(photo d)**.

Fringe dangles

[1] Cut a 1½-in. (3.8cm) piece of 24-gauge wire. Fold over the tip to make a head pin **(photo e)**.

[2] String a 3mm color A bead and make a wrapped loop above the bead (Basics and **photo f**).

[3] Repeat steps 1 and 2 to make a total of 18 color A dangles.

[4] Repeat steps 1 and 2 to make a total of nine 3mm B dangles, making only the first half of a wrapped loop above the beads **(photo g)**.

[5] Repeat steps 1 and 2 to make a total of 10 3mm C dangles, making only the first half of a wrapped loop.

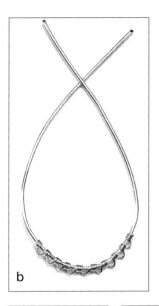

b

c

d

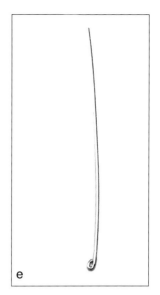

e

f

g

h

i

j

k

l

EDITOR'S NOTE:

Making the loops at the bottom of the earring is the trickiest part of this project. Practice with copper or craft wire until you're comfortable with the technique.

[6] Slide an A dangle into the loop of a B dangle (photo h). Repeat until you've connected all the A dangles to a B or C dangle. You'll have one C dangle left over.

[7] Cut a 2-in. (5cm) piece of 24-gauge wire and fold the tip over to make a head pin. String a 6mm round bead or an 8mm rondelle, a spacer, and a 3mm B. Make the first half of a wrapped loop (photo i). Make a total of two round/rondelle accent dangles.

[8] Make one dangle with a teardrop, a spacer, and one or two Cs as in step 7 (photo j).

Center dangle

[1] Cut a 2½-in. (6.4cm) piece of 24-gauge wire and make a wrapped loop at one end. Slide this loop into the loop of a C dangle from step 6 and finish the wraps.

[2] String an 8mm round crystal, a spacer, and a teardrop. Make a wrapped loop above the beads.

Assembly

[1] Attach the teardrop dangle from step 8 of "Fringe dangles" to the middle loop on the nine-loop segment and finish the wraps. Skip a loop on either side and attach one of the round/rondelle dangles to each.

[2] Attach a B and a C dangle to each side of the teardrop accent dangle, and finish the wraps. Repeat for the round/rondelle accent dangles (photo k). Attach a B and a C dangle to each remaining loop.

[3] Cut a 2-in. piece of 24-gauge wire and wrap one end three times around the wire frame about ½ in. (1.3cm) from the top.

[4] String two 3mm As, the center dangle, and two 3mm As. Wrap the wire around the other side of the frame. Trim the excess (photo l).

[5] Open the loop on an earring finding and attach the earring. Close the loop.

[6] Make a second earring.

Lovely lines

Give yourself a classic look with these stylish earrings

designed by **Lilian Chen**

MATERIALS

- **8** gemstone or glass rondelles, **2–4** each of **2–4** graduated sizes
- 2 ft. (61cm) 22-gauge wire, half-hard
- **2** 6mm jump rings
- pair of earring findings
- chainnose pliers
- roundnose pliers
- wire cutters

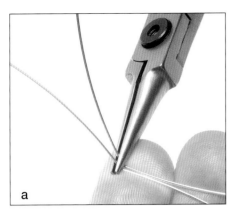

a

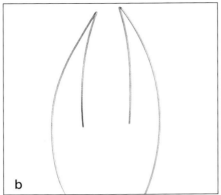

b

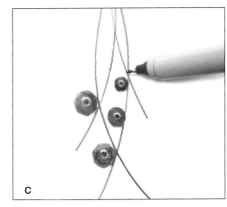

c

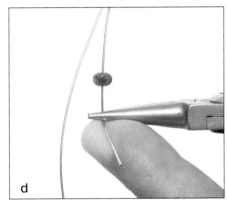

d

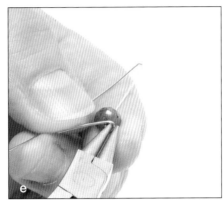

e

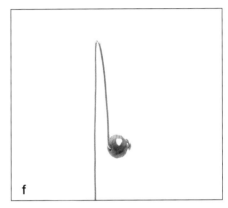

f

The natural curve of wire lends itself to these stylized leaves. Work with two wires at once to create a perfectly matched pair of earrings.

stepbystep

[1] Without distorting the natural curve of the wire, cut four 6-in. (15cm) pieces of wire.

[2] On one wire, make a mark 2 in. (5cm) from one end. Repeat with another wire. These will be called A wires. On a third wire, make a mark 2½ in. (6.4cm) from one end. Repeat with the remaining wire. These two wires will be B wires. You will use an A and a B for each earring, but to make the bends symmetrical, you'll work the As together and the Bs together.

[3] Position the two As so the marks are side by side and the wires curve in opposite directions. Grasp the wires with chainnose pliers at the marks, and bend them together (photo a). Fold them all the way over so the ends are going in roughly the same direction. When

the bend is complete, you'll have two symmetrical pieces, one for the left earring, one for the right (photo b).

[4] Repeat step 3 with the two B wires.

[5] Hang an A and a B on a piece of scrap wire, and carefully set it down. Temporarily arrange the beads near the spots where the wires intersect each other. I designed my earrings with the two smaller beads on the A wires and the two larger beads on the B wires. Mark each bead placement spot with a permanent marker (photo c).

[6] Measure ¾ in. (1.9cm) from each bead placement mark, and trim the end. This will give you enough wire to make two spirals on the front of each bead.

[7] String a bead on one of the wire ends, and make a right-angle bend at the bead placement mark (photo d). Use roundnose and chainnose pliers to make a flat spiral with the ¾-in. (1.9cm) tip

(photo e). Position the bead against the coil, and make another right-angle bend to hold the bead in place (photo f).

[8] Repeat step 7 with the other three wire ends.

[9] Open a jump ring (Basics), and attach the two wires and an earring finding.

[10] Repeat steps 5–9 with the other two wires.

EDITOR'S NOTE:

This project can be challenging because any inadvertent movement causes unwanted bends in the wire. Practice with craft wire before trying gold or silver, but harden your practice wire first to approximate the stiffness of half-hard wire. (To harden the wire, grasp each end with pliers. Hold one end still, and pull the other end while twisting it back and forth.)

Paisley
perfection

The perfect lines and curls of
these earrings are an ideal
finishing touch for any outfit

designed by **Sonia Kumar**

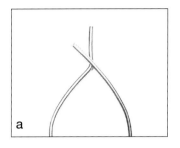 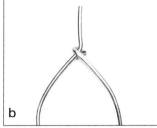  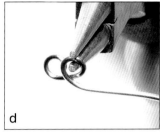

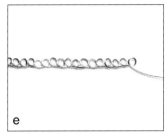 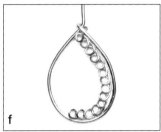 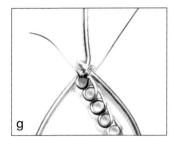 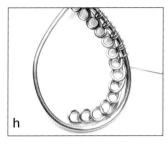

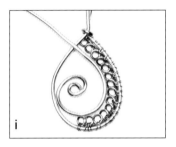  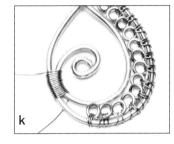 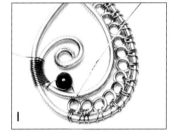

Add gemstones to wire frames for earrings reminiscent of motifs found in Persian artwork.

stepbystep

[1] Cut 5 in. (13cm) of 16-gauge wire, and bend it from the center to form a teardrop shape, overlapping the ends. Bend one end so it points straight up **(photo a)**. Wrap the other end around the vertical end, and trim **(photo b)**.
[2] Cut 9 in. (23cm) of 20-gauge wire, and make a plain loop at one end with roundnose pliers **(photo c)**. Reposition the roundnose pliers next to the previous loop, and wrap the long wire around the pliers to make another loop **(photo d)**. Repeat to make a continuous series of loops **(photo e)** that is long enough to fit about halfway around the inside of the teardrop frame. Decrease the size of the last few loops in the series. Trim the end, and place the series of loops in the teardrop frame **(photo f)**.
[3] Cut about 12 in. (30cm) of 28-gauge wire, and wrap it a few times around the first loop and the teardrop frame **(photo g)**. Continue along the edge of the teardrop, connecting the loops to the frame **(photo h)**. Trim the ends, and press them close to your work.
[4] Cut 5 in. (13cm) of 16-gauge wire, and make a simple loop at one end. Hold the loop flat with chainnose pliers, and make an open spiral that will fit within the teardrop frame **(photo i)**. Trim the end **(photo j)**.
[5] Cut 24 in. (61cm) of 28-gauge wire, and begin wrapping it around the teardrop frame and the spiral **(photo k)**.
[6] Wrap the wire once around the spiral wire only. String a 4mm gemstone bead onto the 28-gauge wire, and wrap the wire around the spiral and the nearest loop **(photo l)**. Continue connecting the spiral to the loops, adding 4mms at regular intervals, until you've added seven 4mms and reached the top of the frame. Trim the wire, and press the end close to your work.
[7] Using roundnose pliers, make a simple loop with the remaining wire end at the top of the frame **(photo m)**.
[8] Open the loop (Basics) of an earring wire, attach it to the loop made in step 7, and close the loop.
[9] Make a second earring as the mirror image of the first.

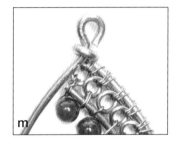

MATERIALS

- **14** 4mm round gemstone beads
- 20 in. (51cm) 16-gauge wire, dead-soft
- 18 in. (46cm) 20-gauge wire
- 2 yd. (1.8 m) 28-gauge wire
- pair of earring findings
- chainnose pliers
- roundnose pliers
- wire cutters

WIREWORK & CHAIN MAIL

81

Ruffled rings

Create colorful dangling earrings from layered jump ring clusters

designed by **Sandy Amazeen**

MATERIALS

- **2–6** 6–8mm crystals (optional)
- **12–14** 6º or 8º seed beads (optional)
- **2–6** 2-in. (5cm) 20-gauge head pins or eye pins (optional)
- jump rings
  - **14** 4.25mm inside diameter stainless steel or brass, 18-gauge
  - **84** anodized aluminum in assorted colors sizes/wire gauges
- pair of earring findings
- bentnose pliers
- chainnose pliers
- roundnose pliers (optional)
- wire cutters (optional)

DESIGNER'S NOTE:

If closing the base jump ring is difficult, remove one of the colored rings, and close the base jump ring. Open the colored jump ring, and slide it through the base jump ring.

A sample bag of mixed anodized aluminum jump rings inspired Sandy to modify a simple chain mail pattern known as Shaggy Loops. A clustered effect results from combining jump rings in different sizes and wire gauges. Beads and crystals add extra sparkle to the jump rings and earring findings, and it's easy to match the earrings to any piece of clothing.

stepbystep

You can make these earrings from any combination of jump rings — vary the jump ring size, wire gauge, and color. Customize them even more by changing the length, dangling crystals or beads from the bottom, or embellishing the jump rings with seed beads. Follow

these basic instructions, and modify them as desired.

[1] For each earring, you will need seven 4.25mm stainless steel or brass jump rings for the base chain, and three sets of 14 rings in different sizes, wire gauges, and/or colors. Select your jump rings, and lay them on your work surface in rows with the base jump rings

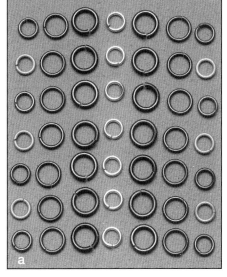

EDITOR'S NOTE:
If you use smaller jump rings of a finer wire gauge, you will need to stack more jump rings on each side of the base jump ring to fill it out.

in the middle and symmetrical rows on each side (photo a).

[2] Open the seven base jump rings and close the remaining jump rings (Basics). If you plan to attach a seed bead to any of the jump rings, embellish them before closing the jump rings (photo b).

[3] If you plan to attach dangles to the bottom of the earrings, make them now. To make a dangle, string a 6mm crystal on a head or eye pin. Note the size of the bottom jump ring before making a plain loop (Basics). Make the loop large enough

to fit around the jump ring. Vary the length of the dangles if you are adding more than one. Slide the bottom base jump ring through the plain loops before you attach the sets of jump rings (photo c).

[4] Attach a set of closed jump rings to an open base jump ring in the order they were placed on your work surface, working from the center outward (photo d). Close the base jump ring.

[5] Slide an open base jump ring through the top of the closed base jump ring. Attach the sets of closed jump

rings on each side of the base jump ring. Close the base jump ring (photo e).

[6] Repeat step 5 with the remaining open base jump rings.

[7] Attach an earring finding to the top base jump ring (photo f).

[8] Make a second earring.

Square wire, naturally

Wirework leaves display natural charm

designed by **Lilian Chen**

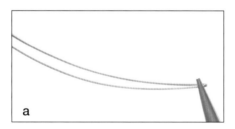

a

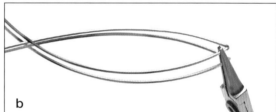

b

The key to creating these earrings is making both pieces at once. Matching bends mean the leaves perfectly mirror one another. Lilian's design was inspired by tiny pine cone charms she found at a bead show, but they'd look just as great with other dangles in the center.

stepbystep

Earring frames

[1] Locate the center point of a 20-in. (51cm) piece of 18-gauge wire. Orient the wire so it forms a large U. Making sure not to twist the wire, use chainnose pliers to grip the wire at the center point. Fold both sides of the U over the jaws of the pliers to make a symmetrical curve **(photo a)**.

[2] Orient the folded wire like a U. Using chainnose pliers, grasp both halves of the wire 4 in. (10cm) from the first fold. Make a sharp bend **(photo b)** toward the ends of the wire, positioning the fold between the two halves of the wire.

[3] Reposition your chainnose pliers 1/16 in. (2mm) above the bend you just made. Gripping both halves, bend them up 15 degrees as you push the pliers down **(photo c)**. This will create a slight kink.

[4] Form the leaf shapes as desired. To create a more pronounced curve than the wire has naturally, position your pliers in the bend and hold both halves of the wire between your index finger and thumb. Pull up slightly with your finger as you push

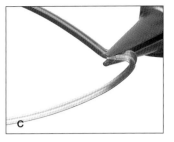

c

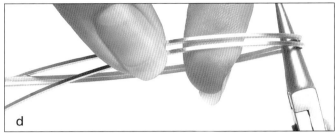

d

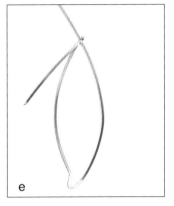

e

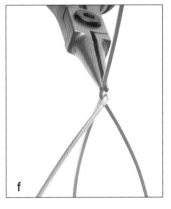

f

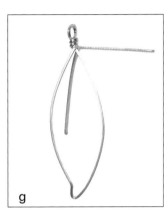

g

h

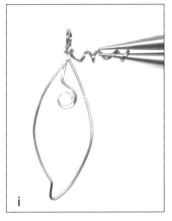

i

j

MATERIALS

- 2 15–18mm metal charms
- 20 in. (51cm) 18-gauge square sterling silver or gold-filled wire, dead-soft
- 2 jump rings
- pair of earring findings
- chainnose pliers
- roundnose pliers
- wire cutters

EDITOR'S NOTE:

Crystal pendant beads lend a new look to these earrings. To make a pendant bead hang correctly, string it on 3 in. (7.6cm) of wire, and make a set of wraps above it as for a top-drilled bead (Basics). Make the first half of a wrapped loop (Basics), slide the loop through the center coil, and finish the wraps.

down with your thumb, and gently "walk" your fingers in this position along the length of the wires (photo d). Repeat until your wire has the desired amount of curve. When 1 in. (2.5cm) of the shorter wire section overlaps the longer section, clip the wire apart at the first bend. You now have two leaf shapes.

[5] On one leaf shape, grip the shorter wire end with chainnose pliers, and bend it over the longer end (photo e).

[6] Grip the longer wire end just above the shorter end, and bend the longer end slightly against its curve (photo f).

[7] Using roundnose pliers, grip the longer wire end 1/16 in. (2mm) above the shorter end, and create a wrapped loop (Basics and photo g). Do not trim the excess wire.

[8] Using roundnose pliers, form an open-center coil with the shorter end, positioning the coil within the leaf shape (photo h). Create curves in the coil's wire, using roundnose pliers.

[9] Using roundnose pliers, form a loose spiral with the longer wire end (photo i).

[10] Adjust the loops of the spiral so that it falls adjacent to the leaf shape. Using

roundnose pliers, create a small loop at the end of the spiral. Attach the loop to the leaf shape, and pinch it closed with chainnose pliers (photo j).

[11] Repeat steps 5–10 with the other wire to make a matching earring in the mirror image of the first.

Assembly

[1] Open a jump ring (Basics). Use it to attach a charm to the open-center coil of an earring, and close the jump ring.

[2] Open the loop of an earring finding. Attach an earring and close the

loop. If necessary, rotate the loop of the earring finding so that the leaf faces forward. Repeat for the second earring.

Delicate drops

Paint the town red with contemporary wire earrings

designed by **Jane Konkel**

Garnets appear in jewelry throughout history and in particular enjoyed a surge of popularity in the Victorian era. These stunning little dangles showcase garnets' warm glow, but Czech glass beads can be used as a lower-budget substitute, if necessary.

MATERIALS
- **10** 4mm garnet beads
- **12 in.** (30cm) 20-gauge half-hard wire
- **10** 1½-in. (3.8cm) decorative head pins
- **2** 5mm jump rings
- pair of earring findings
- chainnose pliers
- roundnose pliers
- wire cutters
- bench block or anvil
- hammer

a

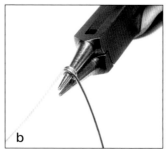

b

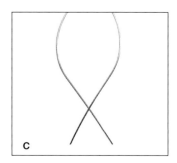

c

d

e

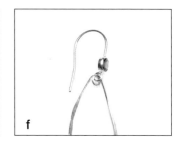

f

stepbystep

[1] On a decorative head pin, string a garnet bead. Make a wrapped loop (Basics). If desired, make additional wraps around the top of the bead **(photo a)**. Make a total of five bead units.
[2] Cut a 6-in. (15cm) piece of 20-gauge wire. Position your roundnose pliers at the center of the wire. Pull both ends of the wires around the pliers' top jaw **(photo b)**.
[3] Pull each end down to form an X **(photo c)**.
[4] Use roundnose pliers to form a coil on each end of the wire. On a bench block or anvil, hammer both sides of the wire while gently pinching it together **(photo d)**.
[5] Open a jump ring (Basics). Attach one coil, the bead units, and the remaining coil. Close the jump ring **(photo e)**.
[6] Open the loop of an earring wire (Basics). Attach the dangle and close the loop **(photo f)**.
[7] Make a second earring.

Contributors

Contact former *Bead&Button* editor **Ann Dee Allen** in care of Kalmbach Books.

Sandy Amazeen resides in Williams, Ariz., where she dreams up new bead and wirework designs when she's not busy hiking or rock hounding. Contact her at amamess@earthlink.net.

Contact former *Bead&Button* associate editor **Tea Benduhn** in care of Kalmbach Books.

Kimberly Berlin is a full-time jewelry artist, teaches wireworking classes in San Antonio, Texas, and is the author of *Build Your Own Wire Pendants*. Contact her at berlik@flash.net.

Kathy Budda has been designing jewelry since 2007, and works at Nottingham Beads in Delafield, Wis. Contact Kathy through the store at nottinghambeads.com.

Lilian Chen is an internationally known bead and wire artist whose designs have been featured in several beading magazines. Lilian was named a Swarovski Create Your Style Ambassador in 2009. Visit community.create-your-style.com/user/51489/goldgatsby to view Lilian's designs, or contact her at lilian888crystals@yahoo.com.

Jane Danley Cruz is an associate editor of *Bead&Button* magazine. Contact her at jcruz@beadandbutton.com.

Gail Damm owns Bead Haven stores in Frankenmuth, Mich., and Las Vegas, Nev. She loves teaching beading classes and using crystals in her designs. Contact her at 702-233-2450 or 989-652-3566, via email at lasvegas@beadhaven.com, or visit beadhaven.com.

Anna Elizabeth Draeger is a former associate editor at *Bead&Button* magazine and author of *Crystal Brilliance* and *Great Designs for Shaped Beads*. Visit http://originaldesignsbyanna.squarespace.com.

Julia Gerlach is editor of *Bead&Button* magazine. Contact her at jgerlach@kalmbach.com.

Gloria Farver has been beading since 2000. In addition to beading, she also enjoys knitting, gardening, and spending time with family and friends. Contact Gloria at rod_farver@yahoo.com.

Melanie Hazen lives in Cumberland City, Tenn., and has been making jewelry for several years. Visit melaniehazen.etsy.com.

Valerie Hector has spent a great deal of time studying the history of Chinese beadwork. Visit valeriehector.com, or email her at valerie@valeriehector.com.

Bethany Heywood has been beading since 2002 and loving every sparkly minute of it. Contact her at beth.heywood@gmail.com.

Cathy Jakicic is editor of *Bead Style* magazine and the author of *Hip Handmade Memory Jewelry* and *Jewelry Projects from a Beading Insider*. She has been creating jewelry for more than 15 years. Contact her at cjakicic@beadstyle.com.

Virginia Jensen is the author of *Cube Bead Stitching* and *Contemporary Cube Bead Designs*. With many years of design experience, it's no surprise that her greatest joy in beadwork is the design process. She lives in Grand Junction. Colo. Visit her website, virjenmettle.com.

Amy Johnson draws inspiration from her background in tapestry weaving and graphic design to create her beaded jewelry. Three of her pieces have been finalists in the annual Bead Dreams competition. Email her at amy@amyjohnsondesigns.com, or visit amyjohnsondesigns.com.

Contact former *Art Jewelry* associate editor **Addie Kidd** in care of Kalmbach Books.

Contact **Cyndy Klein** in care of Kalmbach Books.

Jane Konkel is associate editor of *Bead Style*. Contact her at jkonkel@beadstyle.com.

Sonia Kumar began making jewelry with paper clips in 2004. She now works mainly with wire and gemstones. Visit catchalljewelry.etsy.com.

Laura Landrum has beaded since 1992, and loves experimenting with different styles of beaded beads. Contact her at landrumjewelry@gmail.com, or visit lauralandrum.biz.

Glorianne Ljubich began beading 10 years ago and quickly fell under its spell. Incorporating beadweaving, wireworking, and stringing, she designs and teaches in Seattle, Wash. Contact her at info@fusionbeads.com.

Melody MacDuffee is a fiber and wire jewelry artist from Mobile, Ala. The author of several beading books including *Lacy Wire Jewelry*, she also directs Soul of Somanya, a nonprofit organization that offers living-wage employment to young West African artisans. Visit soulofsomanya@gmail.com.

Beadweaver **Rachel Nelson-Smith** teaches internationally and at her monthly Bead Salon in Santa Cruz, Calif. Contact her at contact@rachelnelsonsmith.com, or visit rachelnelsonsmith.com.

Contact **Julie Olah** in care of Kalmbach Books.

Glenda Paunonen is the owner, educator, and creative director of Crystal Creations Bead Institute/Beads Gone Wild, in West Palm Beach, Fla. Contact her at 561-649-9909, via email at info@beadsgonewild.com, or visit her website, beadsgonewild.com.

Kristin Schneidler is a writer and editor from the Milwaukee, Wis., metro area. She lives with her husband and two sons and enjoys crafts when she can find the time. Contact Kristin in care of Kalmbach Books.

Jennifer Schwartzenberger is the owner of Stony Creek Bead in Ypsilanti, Mich., where she spends all day helping others become as addicted to beading as she is. Contact her at 734-544-0904, or visit stonycreekbead.blogspot.com.

Sherry Serafini is an award-winning beadwork artist and coauthor of *The Art of Bead Embroidery*, *Sensational Bead Embroidery*, and *Beading Across America*. She was voted one of the Top Ten Teachers by *Bead&Button* magazine in 2011. Creativity is key to her pieces, and she encourages others to take liberty when working with her designs. Visit serafinibeadedjewelry.com.

Lynne Soto teaches bead jewelry making to individuals and groups through her business, Lessons with Lynne, as well as at the Bead&Button Show. Contact her at mscalto2@att.net.

Liz Stahl, a bead hobbyist who enjoys creating with seed beads in her free time, lives in Chelmsford, Mass. She has been beading since 2006. Contact Liz at liz.stahl@comcast.net.

Katia Trebeau lives in Guadelupe, in the French West Indies. Contact her at ericka.trebeau@orange.fr.

Lesley Weiss is the author of *The Absolute Beginners Guide: Stitching Beaded Jewelry* and a former associate editor for *Bead&Button* magazine. Visit homemade-handmade.net.

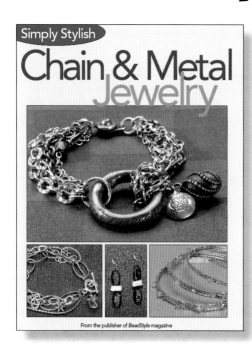

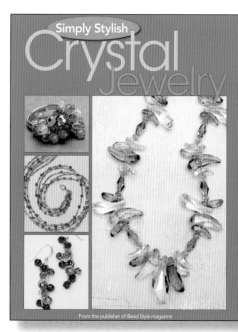